Adviser: Robert Pressling
Designer: Ben White
Editors: Nicola Barber, Annabel Warburg, Catherine Bradley
Picture Research: Elaine Willis

Kingfisher Books, Grisewood and Dempsey Ltd.
Elsley House, 24–30 Great Titchfield Street,
London W1P 7AD

First published in 1991 by Kingfisher Books.
The material published in this edition was previously published in paperback by Kingfisher Books in four separate volumes – Fun With Simple Science: Floating and Sinking, Shadows and Reflections, Machines and Movement, Sound and Music in 1990.

British Library Cataloguing in Publication Data
Taylor, Barbara
    100 simple science experiments.
    1. Science. Experiments
    I. Title
    507.24
ISBN 0-86272 749-9

Phototypeset by Southern Positives and Negatives (SPAN), Lingfield, Surrey
Colour separations by Scantrans pte Ltd., Singapore and Newsele Litho, Milan

Printed in Spain

KINGFISHER

100 SIMPLE SCIENCE EXPERIMENTS

BARBARA TAYLOR

Kingfisher Books

CONTENTS

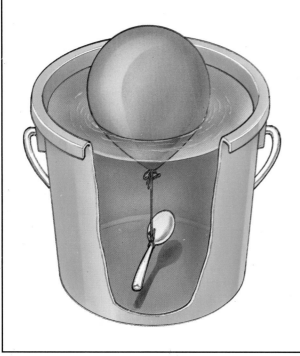

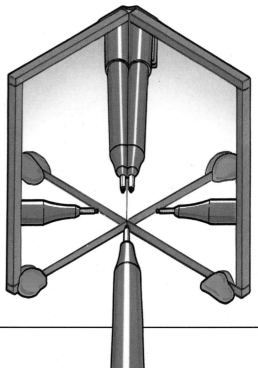

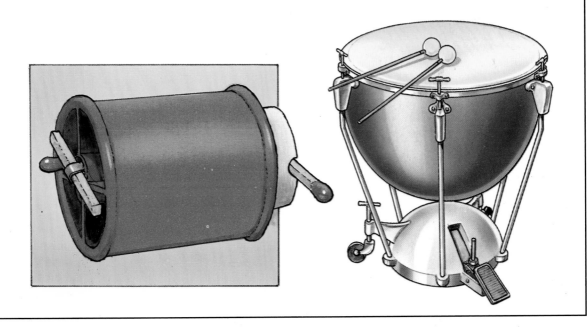

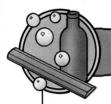

ABOUT THIS BOOK

This book is all about discovering how and why things happen in the world around you. It takes a closer look at ordinary objects, such as scissors, spoons, elastic bands and balloons. It also looks at activities, from bicycling and sailing to playing recorders or bouncing balls. The investigations will help you to understand the importance of simple scientific ideas in your everyday life.

Do not worry if the results of your investigations are not the same as those in the book. Science is all about making new discoveries. It is a good idea to repeat the investigation to check your results and see if you can work out why your results might be different.

Here are some ideas for the kinds of simple materials used in the investigations in this book. You could keep them in a special box so they are easy to find.

scissors, cardboard, modelling clay, paints and brushes, colouring pencils, sticky tape or glue, old boxes or plastic cartons, empty plastic bottles and bowls, torches, cotton reels, aluminium foil, bricks, balsa wood, marbles, string, cloth, balloons, knitting needles, elastic bands, paper clips, newspaper, straws, pins, spoons, buckets.

Hints for Investigations

✳ Before you start, read through the instructions carefully and collect all the materials you need.
✳ Put on some old clothes or wear an apron or an overall.
✳ Clear a space to work on and cover the surface with newspaper or an old cloth.
✳ Take care when cutting things and ask an adult to help you with any difficult or dangerous steps.
✳ When you have finished, clear up any mess you have made and wash your hands.

Floating and Sinking

Why do some things float and other things sink?
What shape are the fastest boats? How do submarines dive
underwater? Why do objects float higher in salty water?
What is the Plimsoll line? Why does oil float on water?
How do you make marbled paper? How deep underwater
can whales dive?

This section will help you to discover the answers to these
questions and has lots of ideas for ways to investigate
floating and sinking.

FLOATING AND SINKING

In this section, you can discover what makes things float or sink and find out how to design the fastest boat.

The section is divided into seven different topics. Look out for the big headings with a circle at each end – like the one at the top of this page. These headings tell you where a new topic starts.

Pages 12–19

Does it Float or Sink?

Shapes and sizes of floaters and sinkers; materials they are made from; displacement.

Pages 20–27

Boat Shapes

Streamlining; keels; carrying cargo; masts; sails.

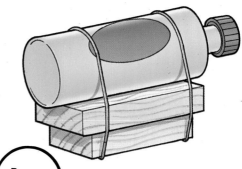

Pages 28–33

Bottles and Balloons

Hollow objects; submarines.

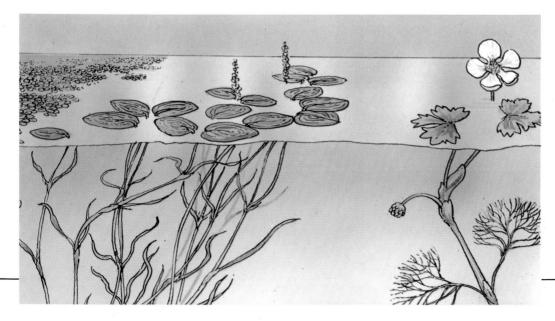

DOES IT FLOAT OR SINK?

Look at the objects along the edges of these two pages.
Which objects will float in water? Which will sink?

Make your own collection of objects to test. Choose
things that are different shapes, sizes and weights. Try to
find things made from different materials, such as paper,
wood or plastic.

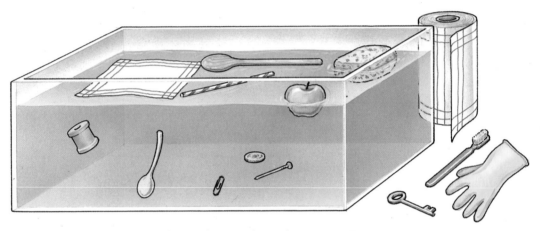

Fill a large bowl, a tank or the bath with water. Put your
collection of objects into the water one at a time. Before
you put each object into the water, see if you can guess
whether it will float or sink.

▶ Next time you are at the seaside or near a lake or a river,
look carefully at any boats floating on the water. Which
materials are they made from? What shape are they? You can
find out more about boats on pages 20–27.

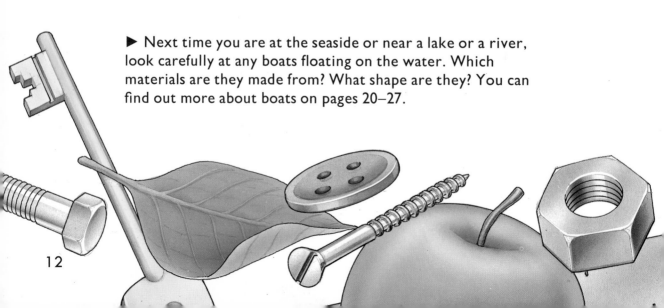

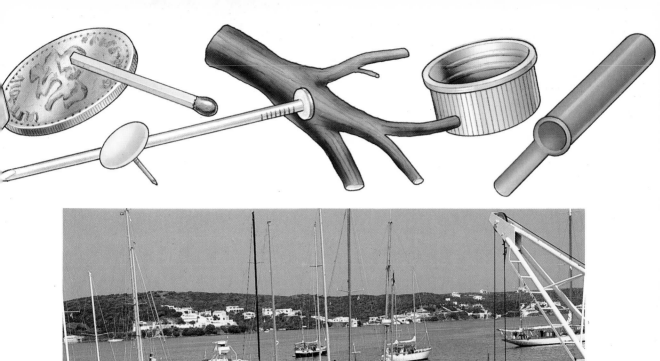

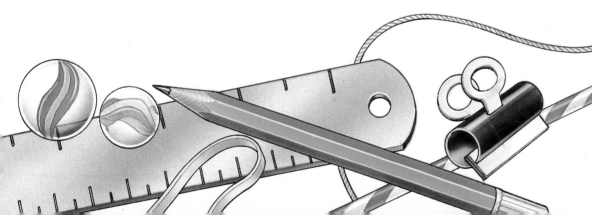

Floaters and Sinkers

To keep a record of the floaters and sinkers you discover, you could draw a chart like this one.

Floaters

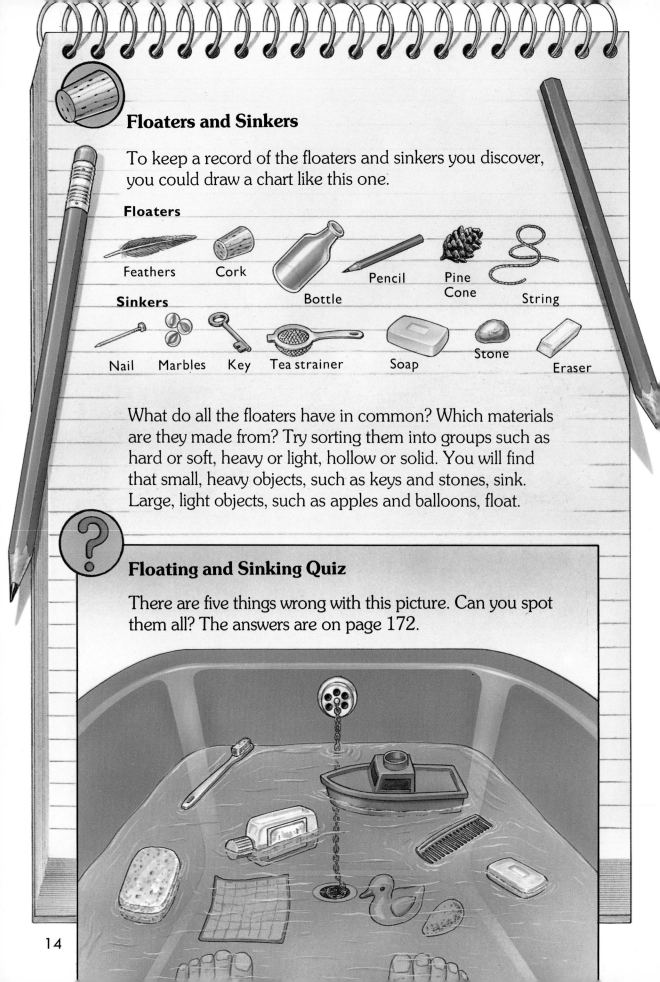

Feathers   Cork   Bottle   Pencil   Pine Cone   String

Sinkers

Nail   Marbles   Key   Tea strainer   Soap   Stone   Eraser

What do all the floaters have in common? Which materials are they made from? Try sorting them into groups such as hard or soft, heavy or light, hollow or solid. You will find that small, heavy objects, such as keys and stones, sink. Large, light objects, such as apples and balloons, float.

Floating and Sinking Quiz

There are five things wrong with this picture. Can you spot them all? The answers are on page 172.

14

Making Floaters Sink

Did you find any objects that sometimes float and sometimes sink? For example, a paper towel floats at first but it soon soaks up the water and sinks. A limpet shell floats one way up but if you turn it over, it sinks. This photograph shows a submersible. When parts of it are filled with water, it sinks below the surface.

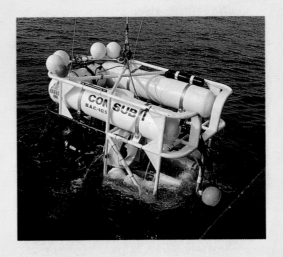

Sponge

The air holes in a sponge make it float high out of the water. Squeeze the sponge under the water. Can you see bubbles of air coming out of the sponge? When you let go of the squeezed sponge, how high does it float?

Tiny holes in the peel of a lemon contain air bubbles. The air makes the lemon float in water. But if you peel a lemon, it sinks! Try peeling an apple. Does this make the apple sink?

Lemon

Peeled lemon

Turn to page 28 to find out more about things filled with air.

Floaters

Sort your floaters into groups according to the materials they are made from. You should use groups such as wood, plastics, rubber, fabrics (wool, cotton, string and so on).

Does all Wood Float?

Collect some different types of wood, such as oak, balsa wood, mahogany, pine, deal and ebony. A timber merchant may let you have small pieces. Put the wood into a bowl of water. Use blocks of wood which are about the same size.

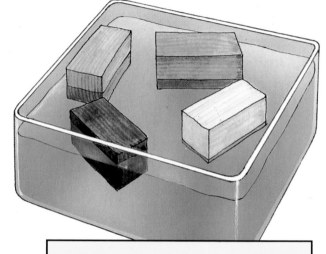

▼ In some countries, tree trunks from the forest float down a river to reach the saw mill.

What happens
You will find that the different types of wood float at different levels in the water. Balsa wood is very light and floats high out of the water. Ebony is so heavy, it sinks.

Icebergs

Huge lumps of ice floating in the sea are called icebergs. Only about a tenth of an iceberg shows above the surface of the water. This makes icebergs very dangerous to ships.

 Make an Iceberg

You will need:
a balloon, water, a freezer, a ruler, scissors.

1. Fit the balloon over a cold tap and fill it with water.
2. Ask an adult to help you tie the end of the balloon to seal the water inside.
3. Put the balloon inside a plastic bag (without holes) and leave the bag in a freezer overnight.
4. Next morning, take the balloon out of the freezer and use the scissors to cut away the balloon carefully.
5. Put your iceberg in a deep bucket of water. It will float, but only just. How much ice is below the water?

Water Pushes Back

Try to push a tennis ball under the water in a bowl. What can you feel? Then let go. What happens?

It's hard to push the ball under the water because the water pushes back. When you let go of the ball, the water pushes it back to the surface again. The upward push of water is called upthrust. An object floats if the upthrust of the water is strong enough to support its weight.

Try the same experiment with a block of polystyrene or a larger ball, such as a soccer ball. Do you have to push harder? What happens when you let go?

Make a Water Candle

How can a candle stay alight underwater? Try this investigation to find out.

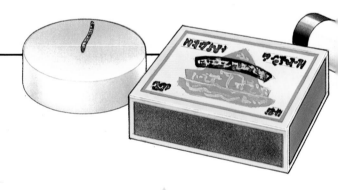

You will need:
a night-light candle, matches, a jar of water, a marker pen.

1. Fill the jar with water almost to the top.
2. Float the candle on the water. Make sure the candle and the wick do not get wet.

Mark water level

Pushing Water out of the Way

Next time you get into a bath, watch the level of the water. To make room for itself, your body pushes some of the water out of the way and the level goes up. This is called displacement. You can use displacement to measure the amount of space your thumb takes up (its volume). You will need a plastic bottle and a measuring jug.

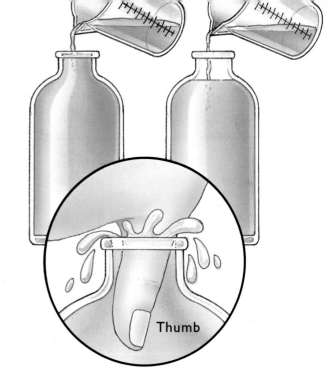

Thumb

1. Fill the bottle with water right up to the top.
2. Stick your thumb into the bottle as far as it will go. Some of the water will spill over the edge.
3. Now use the measuring jug to fill the bottle up to the top again. The amount of water you use to do this is equal to the volume of your thumb.

Wall of wax stops water reaching flame.

What happens

As the candle burns, it gets lighter and floats higher in the water. Because the candle pushes less water up the sides of the jar, the water level goes down.

3. Use the pen to mark the level of the water on the side of the jar.
4. Ask an adult to help you light the candle. Watch what happens. How long does your water candle last?

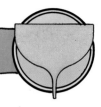

BOAT SHAPES

A ball of modelling clay sinks in water. But if you make the same ball of clay into a boat shape, it floats. The wide, flat boat shape pushes away more water than the narrow, round ball. The water pushes back harder against the flat shape and this holds it up on the surface of the water.

Find the Fastest Shape

Some boats, such as tugboats, are built to be strong and stable, or difficult to tip over. Other boats, such as power boats, are shaped to help them zoom through the water at high speed. This is called a streamlined shape.

Test some boat shapes yourself. Float your boats in a long piece of plastic guttering with two end pieces.

Sample shapes

Cut the boats out of thin balsa wood and use the same amount of wood for each boat.

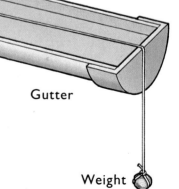

Attach a weight to a long piece of thread and pin the other end of the thread to the front of each boat in turn. Measure the time each boat takes to travel the same distance. Which shape is fastest?

Gutter

Weight

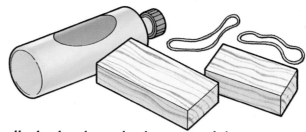

Staying Upright

Some boats have an extra piece called a keel on the bottom of the main body (the hull). To find out how a keel works, make one yourself.

You will need:
an empty plastic bottle, two blocks of wood (one larger than the other), thick elastic bands.

1. Put the bottle into a bowl of water and try tipping it over. You will find that it rolls over quite easily.
2. Now ask an adult to cut two blocks of wood.
3. Use the elastic bands to fix the blocks of wood under the bottle.
4. Float the bottle on the water and try tipping it over again. What happens this time?

What happens
The keel keeps the weight in the centre of the boat and helps it to balance in a level position on the water. It's hard to make the boat tip right over, or capsize.

▼ Keels come in all shapes and sizes. A boat with a keel cannot easily sail in shallow water.

Make a Catamaran

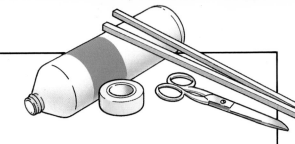

A catamaran is a boat with two hulls. It is a very stable design which will not tip over easily. It does not need a keel to help it stay upright. But if a catamaran does capsize, it's hard to turn it the right way up again.

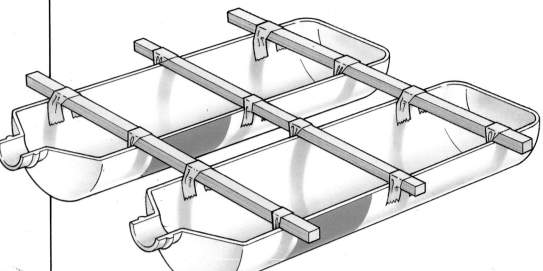

You will need: A washing-up liquid bottle, a small hacksaw, thin strips of balsa wood, waterproof tape, scissors.

1. Ask an adult to cut the washing-up liquid bottle in half with the hacksaw.
2. Use the scissors to cut three narrow strips of balsa wood.
3. Use the tape to stick the balsa wood across the half bottles to match the picture.
4. Try floating your catamaran in water. Can you make it capsize?

Make Metal Ships

You will need:
Tin foil, a block of wood, plastic containers, scissors, sticky tape or glue.

1. Cut a piece of foil larger than the block of wood.
2. Fold it around the wood so the sides stand up. How high do the sides have to be to stop the water getting in? Fix the corners with tape or glue.
4. Line the bottom of your metal boat with more foil.
5. Wrap foil around the plastic containers in the same way.
6. Make some more boats using paper instead of foil. Which boats last longer?

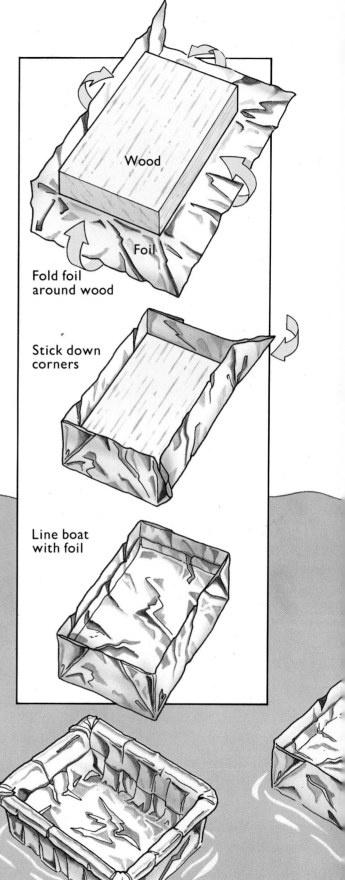

Fold foil around wood

Stick down corners

Line boat with foil

How Much Cargo?

Many boats are made to carry food, cars, books and other kinds of cargo from one place to another. Make some boats out of tin foil and see how much cargo they will carry before they sink. Try boats of different sizes.

Use pieces of thin balsa wood to divide your boats into sections. Load the two end sections with cargo. Or the middle section and one end section. How does this affect the position of the boat?

Fold over the edges all round the boat.

▶ The hold of a container ship is divided into separate sections. This helps to stop the containers moving about as the ship rolls about in rough seas.

Messing about with Masts

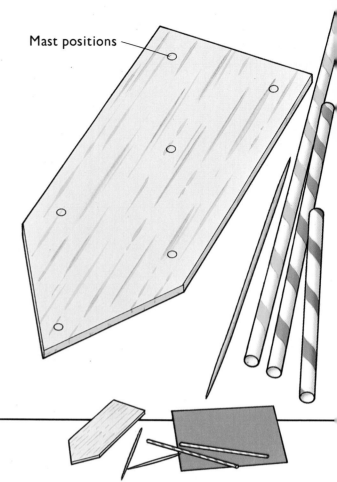

Mast positions

What is the best size and position for the mast on a sailing ship? To find out, cut up some plastic straws to make long, medium length and short masts. Fix each mast in turn onto a balsa wood boat and try tilting the boat to one side. When you let go, does the boat tip over and capsize? Or does it swing back upright again? Put the masts in different positions on the boat.

Super Sails

Make some sails to see how they help a boat to go faster. For the mast, use a straw, a cocktail stick or a piece of thin dowel.

You could make your sails out of paper, cloth or plastic. Blow on each sail or use a paper fan to see which sail makes the boat move fastest. What happens if you blow through a straw on just one side of a sail?

Try different shapes, sizes and numbers of sails.

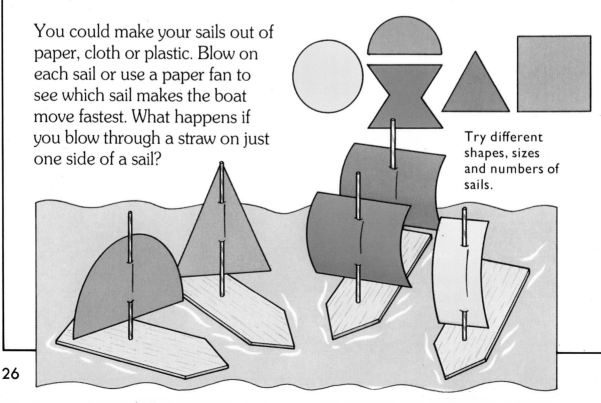

Push a cocktail stick into the balsa wood and slide the straw mast on top.

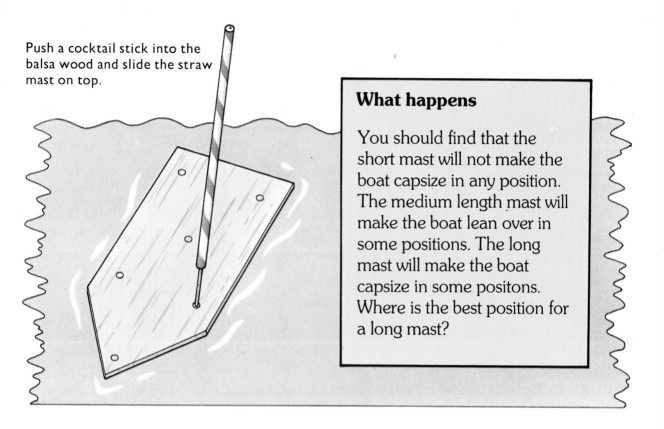

What happens

You should find that the short mast will not make the boat capsize in any position. The medium length mast will make the boat lean over in some positions. The long mast will make the boat capsize in some positons. Where is the best position for a long mast?

▼ How many different kinds of sail can you see on this sailing ship?

BOTTLES AND BALLOONS

Put some hollow objects into a tank or bath of water.
Try some of these: a plastic mug, a plastic bottle, a bowl, a saucepan, an empty drinks can.

You will find that they all float. Can you make any of them sink?

Try pushing them under the water. Look at all the bubbles of air rising to the surface. Even though hollow things look empty, they are really full of air.

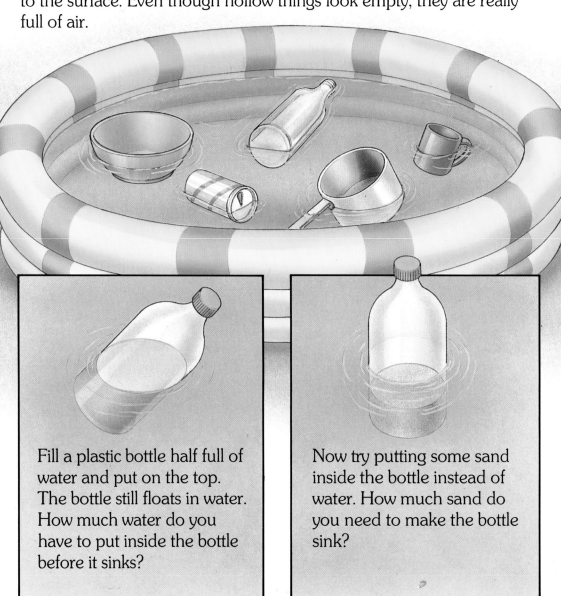

Fill a plastic bottle half full of water and put on the top. The bottle still floats in water. How much water do you have to put inside the bottle before it sinks?

Now try putting some sand inside the bottle instead of water. How much sand do you need to make the bottle sink?

Lifting Buried Treasure

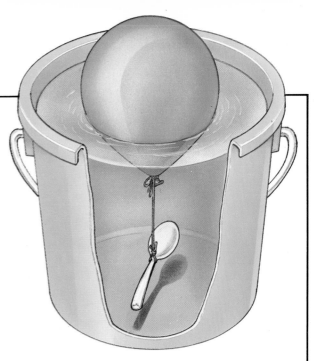

Balloons are full of air so they float high out of the water. If you tie a balloon to a sinker, such as a metal spoon, it will float underneath the balloon. Try different sinkers such as stones, a brick, a mirror, scissors and a screwdriver. Will the balloon lift all these sinkers off the bottom?

▼ Archaeologists use special balloons to lift objects they find on an underwater dig up to the surface.

To find out how submarines dive under the water and rise to the surface again, try these tests.

Rising Raisins

Put some raisins in the bottom of a clear plastic beaker. Fill the beaker half full of a clear, fizzy drink, such as lemonade. Watch what happens.

The raisins will soon zoom up and down the beaker as if by magic. But it's really science, not magic. Can you work out what makes the raisins move? Look at all the bubbles of air that stick to the raisins. How long do the raisins keep rising?

Yellow Submarine

You will need:

a clear jar, a fresh lemon, a balloon, scissors, an elastic band.

1. Use the scissors to cut a piece of lemon peel in the shape of a submarine. Ask an adult for help.
2. Fill the jar with water and put the lemon peel into the water.
3. Cut a circle from the balloon and stretch the balloon over the top of the jar. Hold the balloon in place with the elastic band.

4. When you press hard on the balloon with your finger, you will see your yellow submarine sink down slightly.
5. When you take your finger off the balloon, the submarine will rise up again.

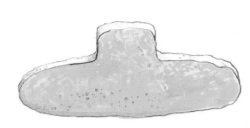

What happens

Air can be easily compressed into a smaller space, but water cannot. As you press on the balloon, you squash the tiny bubbles of air in the lemon peel into a smaller space and let extra water in. This makes the submarine heavier, so it sinks a little . When you take your finger away, the air expands again, pushing out the water. This makes the submarine lighter and it rises up again.

▲ Scientists such as archaeologists, biologists or engineers may use small submarines to help them examine shipwrecks, living things or man-made structures under the sea.

 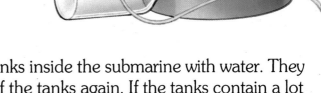

Bottle Submarine

Submarines dive by filling tanks inside the submarine with water. They rise by pumping water out of the tanks again. If the tanks contain a lot of air, the submarine becomes lighter and rises. Make your own submarine to see how this works.

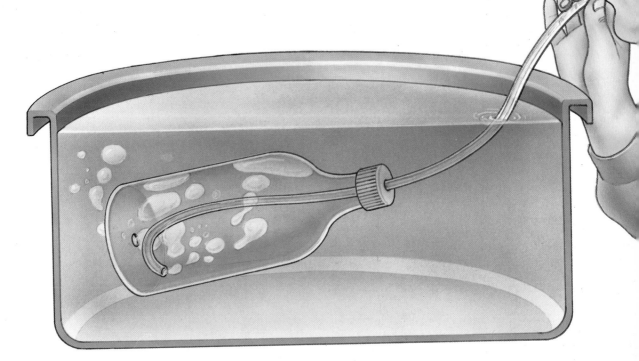

You will need:
a plastic bottle with a lid, a bowl of water, a short length of plastic tubing.

1. Ask an adult to help you make a hole in the lid of the bottle and another hole in the bottom of the bottle.
2. Ask a friend to hold their finger over the hole in the bottom of the bottle and fill it with as much water as you can.

3. Push the tubing through the hole in the bottle top and put the top on the bottle.
4. Lower the bottle carefully into the bowl of water and blow hard down the plastic tube.

What happens

As the air from your lungs goes inside the bottle, it pushes out some of the water. So the bottle rises, just like a real submarine.

33

WATER'S STRETCHY SKIN

Watch water dripping from a tap. There is a special force on the surface of water which pulls it inwards. This force is called surface tension. It gives water drops their smooth, round shape. It also makes water look as if it has a stretchy 'skin' on the surface.

Crazy Colours

Soap or washing-up liquid breaks down the surface tension of water and stops the skin forming. This stops water sticking together in drops and so it flows more easily into all the places where dirt collects. This is one reason why water is better at cleaning things when we add soap or washing-up liquid.

To see what happens when water loses its skin, try this test.

Fill a shallow dish or saucer with milk and put a few drops of food colouring on top of the milk. Use a spoon to drop a small amount of washing-up liquid on top of the colour and watch the colours explode. How long does the swirling movement last? Can you think why it stops?

Food colouring

Spinning Snowman
You will need:
a bowl of water, a cork, thin balsa wood, four cocktail sticks, moth balls, paper, scissors, glue or sticky tape, crayons.

1. Draw and colour a small snowman on the paper and cut it out.
2. Ask an adult to help you cut a slice off the cork. Cut out four small pieces of balsa wood.
3. Stick the snowman to the slice of cork.
4. Make a small notch in each of the small pieces of balsa wood and wedge a piece of moth ball into each notch.
5. Stick the four cocktail sticks into the slice of cork to make a cross shape.
6. Fix the small pieces of balsa wood at the ends of the cocktail sticks.
7. Put your snowman into the bowl of water and watch it spin around.

What happens
The moth balls weaken the pull of the surface tension in the water close to them. The stronger pull of the tension in front of each moth ball pulls the sticks and the snowman around in a circle. How long does the snowman keep spinning?

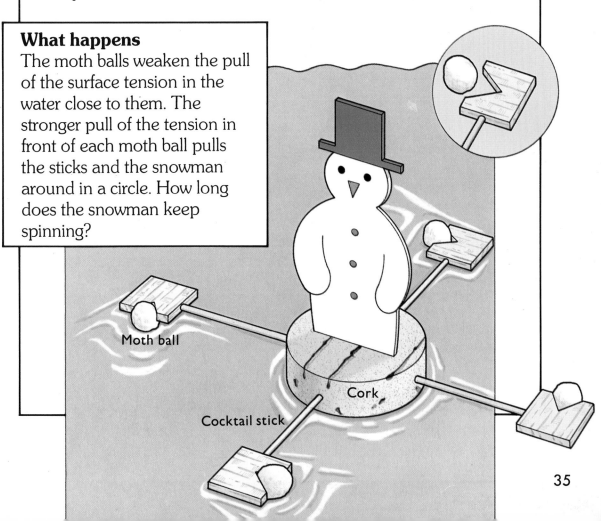

Moth ball

Cork

Cocktail stick

FLOATING LIQUIDS

To measure how things float in different liquids, scientists use an instrument called a hydrometer. The hydrometer sinks farther into some liquids than others. To see how it works, make one yourself.

 Make a hydrometer

Cut about six centimetres off a straw and push a small blob of modelling clay on to the end. Use a thick pencil to mark a line on the straw every five millimetres.

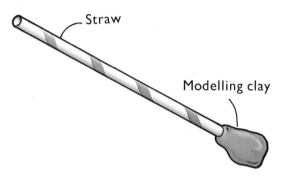

Straw

Modelling clay

Try floating your hydrometer in ordinary water, salty water and surgical spirit. How does it float each time?

Surgical spirit

Tap water

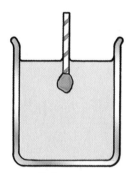

Salt water

What happens

Salty water is heavier than ordinary water so it pushes harder against objects floating in it. To float in salty water, objects need to displace less water than they do in ordinary water. So the hydrometer floats higher in salty water. In surgical spirit, the hydrometer floats at a lower level compared to ordinary water. This shows that surgical spirit is lighter than water.

Salty Surprises

Fresh water

Egg

Salt water

An egg usually sinks in water but this trick shows you how to make an egg look as if it floats in water. First you need to make some very salty water.

1. Pour some warm water into a saucepan and add some salt.

2. Stir with a spoon and keep adding salt until you feel a gritty layer building up on the bottom of the pan.

3. Leave the salty water for several hours until it is no longer cloudy. Then it is ready to use.

4. Half fill a large jar with the salty water and put the egg into the water.

5. Now carefully pour some ordinary tap water down the side of the jar. What happens?

What happens

The tap water is lighter than the salty water so it floats on top. The egg sinks down through the tap water but floats on top of the salty water. It looks as if it is floating in the middle of the jar.

The Plimsoll Line

A ship floats at different levels depending on the weight of the cargo, the temperature of the water and how much salt is in the water. It floats lower in fresh water than in salt water. And it floats lower in warm water than in cold water. The mark called the Plimsoll line shows the safe level for a fully loaded ship in different types of water.

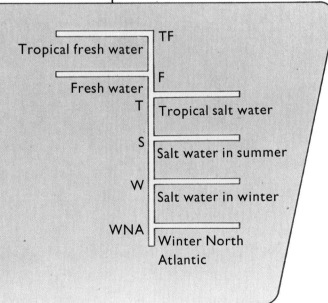

Tropical fresh water — TF

Fresh water — F

T — Tropical salt water

S — Salt water in summer

W — Salt water in winter

WNA — Winter North Atlantic

Rainbow Sandwich

To find out more about how liquids float, make a rainbow sandwich.

Add food colour.

Pour oil down the side of the bottle.

Surgical spirit and food colour

Cooking oil

Water and food colour

You will need:

a tall, thin bottle (such as a test tube, a medicine or perfume bottle or an olive jar), cooking oil, surgical spirit, two different food colours.

1. Fill the bottle about a third full of water and add a few drops of one food colour.
2. Carefully pour oil down the side of the bottle. It will float because oil is lighter than water.
3. Now add a layer of surgical spirit. This is lighter than oil, so it floats on top of the oil. To colour the top of your sandwich, add a few drops of a different food colour.
4. If your bottle has a lid, you can try turning your sandwich upside down. Be careful to keep the surgical spirit and water apart. If they touch each other, they will mix together and you will lose half your sandwich. If this happens, start again.

▶ Workers try to collect oil which floated on top of the sea water until tides and currents washed it on to the beach.

Make a Salad Dressing

Do you know why you have to shake salad dressing before you pour it on a salad? Make some yourself to find out.

You will need:

1 tablespoon vinegar, 2 tablespoons salad oil, $\frac{1}{4}$ level teaspoon salt, some pepper, $\frac{1}{4}$ level teaspoon dry mustard, $\frac{1}{4}$ level teaspoon sugar.

1. Put the salt, pepper, mustard and sugar into a bowl.
2. Pour on the vinegar and stir with a spoon to mix everything together.
3. Add the oil a little at a time. Each time you add more oil, beat the mixture with a fork.
4. Put the salad dressing in a bottle in the fridge.

5. After a while, the dressing will settle into layers. What is the top layer made of?
6. Make sure the lid is tightly on the bottle and shake it hard. What happens to the layers?

What happens

Vinegar contains water, which won't mix with the oil. The oil is lighter than the vinegar so it floats to the top of the bottle and stays there. When you shake the dressing, the oil breaks up into little drops which hang in the vinegar for a while. This makes the dressing look cloudy. How long does the dressing take to go back into layers? If you shake the dressing for longer, can you see any difference in the size of the oil drops?

The Floating Circle

This trick with floating liquids will help you understand more about why things float.

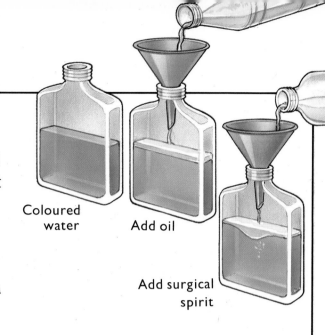

Coloured water   Add oil

Add surgical spirit

You will need:
surgical spirit, cooking oil, green food colouring, water, a funnel, a small, flat bottle.

1. Fill the bottle about half full of water.
2. Add a few drops of green food colouring.
3. Use the funnel to pour a few spoonfuls of oil into the bottle.
4. Now add some surgical spirit and watch how the oily layer bends in the middle.
5. Keep adding the surgical spirit until the oily layer becomes a circle floating in the middle of the green liquids.

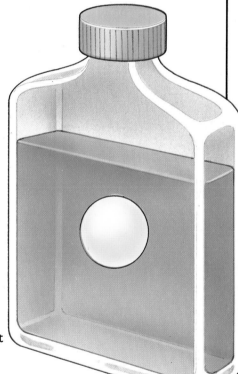

After adding surgical spirit

What happens

When you add the surgical spirit, it mixes with the water and makes the water lighter (less dense). The watery mix pushes up less strongly against the oily layer so the oil starts to sink down into the watery mix. As you add more surgical spirit, the watery mix starts to push on the oil equally from all directions. This makes the oil into the shape of a ball.

Marbling

By floating oily paints or inks on the surface of water, you can make wonderful swirly patterns to decorate paper. This is called marbling because the patterns are like the ones you can see in pieces of polished marble.

You will need:

an old bowl, marbling inks or oil paints, plain paper, a straw or old fork, newspaper. (If you don't have any oil paints, use some powder paint mixed with cooking oil.)

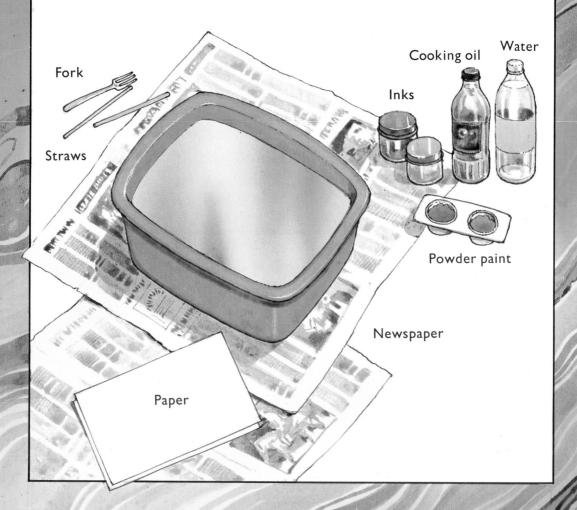

Fork

Straws

Inks

Cooking oil

Water

Powder paint

Newspaper

Paper

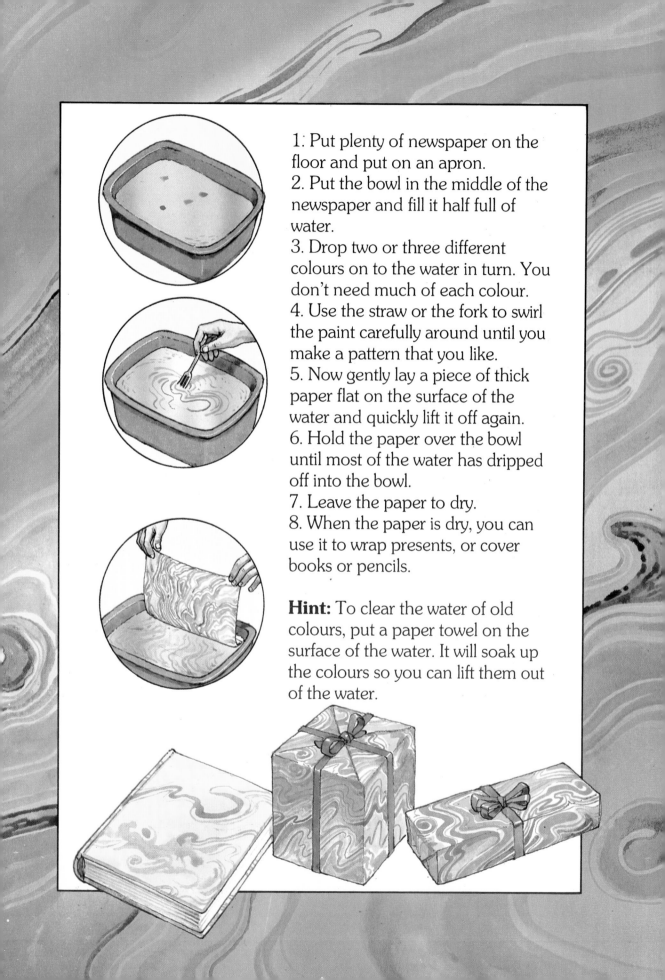

1: Put plenty of newspaper on the floor and put on an apron.

2. Put the bowl in the middle of the newspaper and fill it half full of water.

3. Drop two or three different colours on to the water in turn. You don't need much of each colour.

4. Use the straw or the fork to swirl the paint carefully around until you make a pattern that you like.

5. Now gently lay a piece of thick paper flat on the surface of the water and quickly lift it off again.

6. Hold the paper over the bowl until most of the water has dripped off into the bowl.

7. Leave the paper to dry.

8. When the paper is dry, you can use it to wrap presents, or cover books or pencils.

Hint: To clear the water of old colours, put a paper towel on the surface of the water. It will soak up the colours so you can lift them out of the water.

SINKING TO THE BOTTOM

Rocks such as sandstone are made of layers of small pieces (or particles) of sand. These settle one on top of the other. This often happens underwater when sandy particles washed off the land by rivers sink down to the bottom of an ocean or lake. As more and more sand collects, the weight presses the layers together and squeezes the water out. Over millions of years, the sand becomes hard enough to form rocks.

You can experiment with soil particles to find out more about how rocks form.

Find a large jar with a lid and put in some garden soil until the jar is about one-third full. Fill the rest of the jar with water. Put on the lid, shake the jar and leave it to settle. After a few days, you should be able to see different layers in the jar.

Each layer is made up of particles of a different size. Are the biggest particles on the top or the bottom?

Cleaning Water

The way small particles sink down through water is used to help us clean the water we drink. At the waterworks, the dirty water from rivers and wells goes through big tanks where all the 'bits' sink to the bottom and are taken out. Then the water goes through filters made of sand and gravel. These trap other dirt which sinks down through the water and into the sand.

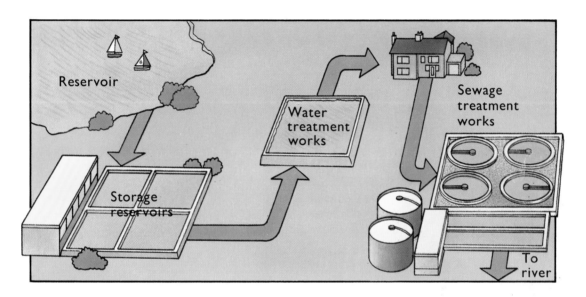

These are filter beds where the dirt is trapped.

PLANTS AND ANIMALS

Marlin

Water wings full of air help us to float.

Marlin can reach speeds of up to 80 kilometres per hour. Their streamlined shape helps them to move quickly through the water.

Divers wear a weight belt so they can rise and sink.

The sperm whale can dive up to about 3000 metres to search for food. But it has to come to the surface to breathe air after an hour or so.

This seaweed has air bladders to help it to float.

Bladderwrack

Sperm whale

Flat duckweed leaves float on the surface.

Pondweed flowers float on the surface but the leaves stay underwater.

Water crowfoot

Water crowfoot has flat, glossy floating leaves and fern-like underwater leaves. The underwater leaves bend easily when the water moves.

Floating Green Stuff

Plants that float on or in water have special shapes and structures to help them survive. Most water plants have lots of air spaces inside them to keep them upright and floating in the water.

You can make your own underwater garden in a large tank or jar. Buy or take cuttings of plants such as duckweed, water crowfoot, eelgrass, arrowhead, salvinia and Canadian pondweed.

TRUE OR FALSE?

1 A peeled lemon floats on water.

2 Nine-tenths of an iceberg shows above the surface of the water.

3 Submarines dive underwater by filling tanks inside the submarine with water.

4 Ships float higher in salt water than in fresh water.

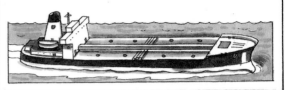

5 Oil floats on water.

6 Sperm whales can stay underwater for ten hours or more.

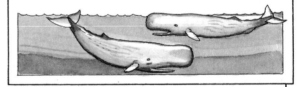

Answers

1 False. A lemon floats only when it has the peel on because air bubbles trapped in the peel make it lighter or less dense.

2 False. Only one-tenth of an iceberg shows above the surface.

3 True.

4 True. In order to float, objects have to displace less salt water than fresh water. This is because salt water is heavier than fresh water and pushes up harder against the objects.

5 True. Oil is lighter or less dense than water so it floats on top of water.

6 False. Sperm whales can stay underwater for only about one hour.

Shadows and Reflections

Why do shadows form? How can you make animal shadows? Can you escape from your shadow? How does the size of shadows change at different times of day? How does a sundial use shadows to tell the time? What is an eclipse? Which materials give the best reflections? How does a periscope work?

This section will help you to discover the answers to these questions and has lots of ideas for ways to investigate shadows and reflections.

SHADOWS AND REFLECTIONS

In this section, you can discover how and why shadows form and take a closer look at the reflections in mirrors and other shiny materials.

The section is divided into five different topics. Look out for the big headings with a circle at each end – like the one at the top of this page. These headings tell you where a new topic starts.

Pages 52–59

Light and Shadows

Transparent, translucent and opaque materials; how light travels; shadow shapes; shadow games.

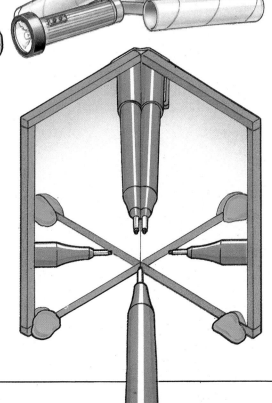

LIGHT AND SHADOWS

Make a collection of objects like the ones along the edges of these two pages. In a dark room, shine a torch on to each object. Which objects let the light through? Which objects keep out the light?

Some things let light go straight through them. You can see clearly through these things. They are said to be transparent. Clear glass and clean water are transparent.

Some things let light through but they scatter the light. If you look through these materials, everything looks blurred. These materials are said to be translucent. Frosted glass and tracing paper are translucent.

Many things do not let any light pass through them. You cannot see through these things. They are said to be opaque. Your body is opaque, so is this book.

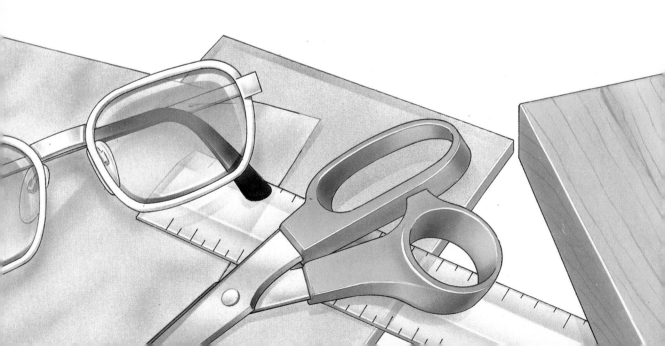

In this picture can you find a transparent material, a translucent material and an opaque material?

53

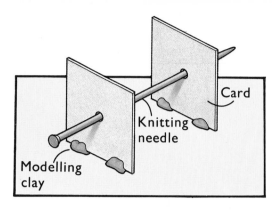

Going Straight

When light hits an opaque object, a dark area forms behind the object. This is called a shadow. Why doesn't light bend round objects and light up the shadow area? To find out, try this test.

1. Cut two pieces of card about 20 centimetres square.
2. To find the middle of the card, draw a line from each corner to the opposite corner. The point where the lines cross is the middle of the card.
3. Cut a hole in the middle of each piece of card.
4. Use modelling clay to fix the

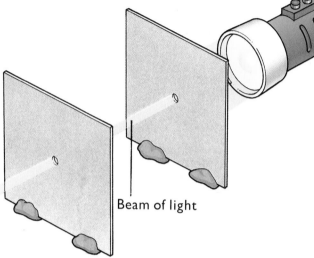

Card

Knitting needle

Modelling clay

Beam of light

Make a Pinhole Camera

To investigate how light travels, try making a pinhole camera.

You will need:
An empty box, thick brown paper, tracing paper, a pin, scissors, sticky tape, black paint, charcoal or a thick black felt pen, a dark cloth or towel.

1. Cut both ends off the box.
2. Paint or colour the inside of the box black.
3. Tape a piece of brown paper over one end of the box.

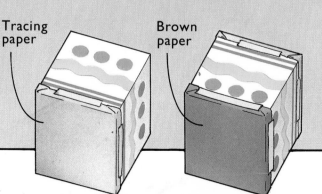

Tracing paper

Brown paper

cards upright about 30 centimetres apart. To line up the holes in a straight line, push a knitting needle through both holes.

5. Ask a friend to shine a light on to the first hole. You should see the light go through the second hole.

6. Now move the second card to one side so the holes are not in a straight line. What happens?

What happens
Light travels in straight lines and cannot bend around things. So when you move the second card out of line, the light cannot get through the second hole.

▲ Can you see the straight edges of these beams of sunlight?

4. Tape a piece of tracing paper over the other end.

5. Use the pin to make a small, round hole in the middle of the brown paper.

6. Cover your head and the tracing paper end of the box with the cloth or towel.

7. Point the camera at a window and look at the tracing paper from about 15 centimetres away. You should see an upside-down window.

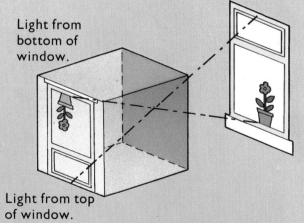

Light from bottom of window.

Light from top of window.

What happens
Light from the top of the window passes in a straight line through the pinhole to the bottom of the tracing paper. Light from the bottom of the window travels to the top of the tracing paper. So the picture you see is upside-down.

Shadow Shapes

Find lots of small objects and see how many different shadow shapes you can make.

A shadow is the same shape as the outside edge of an object. To change the shape of a shadow, move the object around or move the position of the light.

Make a shadow of an object with a hole in the middle. In the shadow, can you make the hole disappear? Try making shadows on different surfaces, such as wood, grass or the stairs. How do the shadows change?

Ask a friend to look only at the shadows of some objects and guess what the objects are. Turn the objects so that the shadows are hard to recognize.

Shadow Portraits

1. Ask a friend to sit sideways on a chair near a wall.
2. Use masking tape to fix a sheet of paper to the wall behind your friend's head.
3. Shine a torch so your friend's head casts a shadow on the paper.
4. Draw around the edge of the shadow with the pencil.
5. Paint inside the outline.

Animal Shadows

With your hands, you can make animal shadows. Here are some ideas. How many more can you discover?

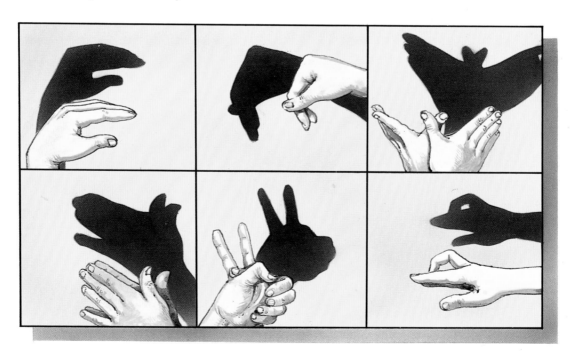

Shadow Games

Can you hide your shadow?
Can you *escape* from your
shadow?

Can you shake hands with a
friend's shadow if your hands are
not touching?

Hide your shadow

Escape from your shadow

Shake hands

Can you catch your friend's shadow? If he is standing on the shadow of a tree or a building, then he is safe and cannot be caught. If you put a foot on his shadow, it's his turn to try and catch your shadow.

Can you make your shadow touch the top of the tree? Or reach into places where you cannot go?

Can you fit inside your friend's shadow?

Can you jump on your friend's shadow?

BIG AND SMALL SHADOWS

Cut out a star shape from a piece of card and fix it to a pencil with modelling clay. Prop up a large piece of white paper on some books. In a dark room, shine a torch on to your star.

Hold the star near the torch.
How big is the shadow?

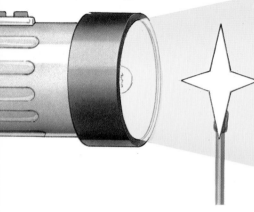

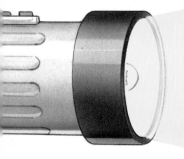

Now move the star farther away from the torch.
What happens to the shadow. Is it bigger or smaller?
What happens to the size of the shadow if you keep the star in one place and move the torch backwards and forwards?

What happens
When the star is near the light, it blocks out a lot of light, so the shadow is big. When the star is farther away from the light, it blocks out less light, so the shadow is smaller.

Long and short shadows

On a sunny day, find a safe area of concrete or asphalt – not out in the street. Ask if you can use chalk to draw around shadows. With a friend, stand in the same place in the early morning, at midday and in late afternoon. Take it in turns to stand still while one of you draws around the other's shadow.

Measure your shadows from head to toe. How does the size of the shadows change at different times of the day? Which direction do your shadows point at different times of the day – north, south, east or west?

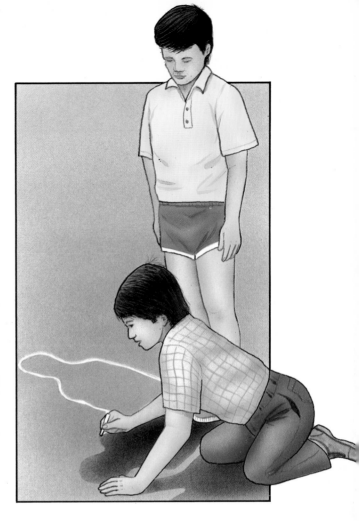

Compare your shadows on a summer's day with your shadows on a day in winter. How are they different?

What happens
In the early morning or late afternoon, the Sun is low in the sky and shadows are long. At midday, the Sun is high above you and your shadows are shorter. In winter, the Sun is lower in the sky than it is in summer. So winter shadows are longer than summer shadows.

You will need: a pencil or a short stick, a cotton reel, glue or modelling clay, a large piece of white paper.

Make a Shadow Clock

You can use shadows to help you tell the time. Here's how to make a shadow clock.

1. Stand a pencil or a short stick in a cotton reel.
2. Use glue or modelling clay to fix the reel to a large piece of white paper.
3. On a sunny day, put your shadow clock out of doors where the Sun will shine on it.
4. Draw a line along the shadow of the stick and write the time at the end of the line.
5. Do the same thing every hour.

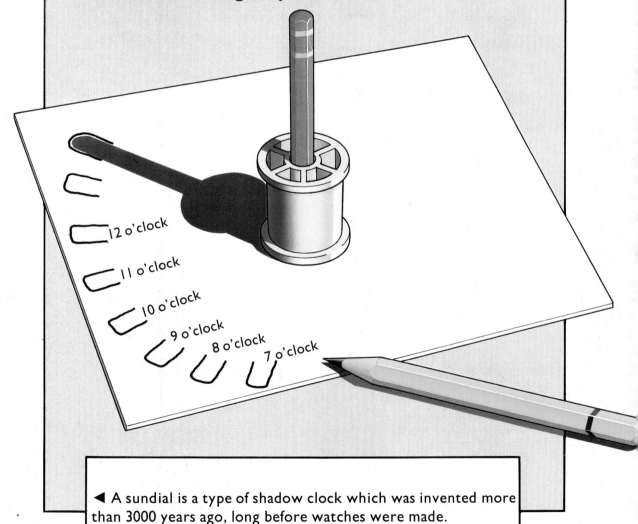

12 o'clock
11 o'clock
10 o'clock
9 o'clock
8 o'clock
7 o'clock

◀ A sundial is a type of shadow clock which was invented more than 3000 years ago, long before watches were made.

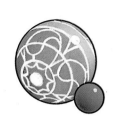

Shadows in Space

The Moon has no light of its own. It shines because it reflects light from the Sun. Sometimes, the Earth moves in a direct line between the Moon and the Sun and stops Sunlight from reaching the Moon. The Earth's shadow makes the Moon look very dark for a while. This is called a Lunar eclipse. 'Lunar' means to do with the Moon.

Try this experiment to see how a Lunar eclipse works.

Use a large beachball or a soccer ball as the Earth and a much smaller ball as the Moon. Stick a piece of string to the 'Moon' so you can hang it in front of the 'Earth'. Use a torch or a table lamp as the Sun.

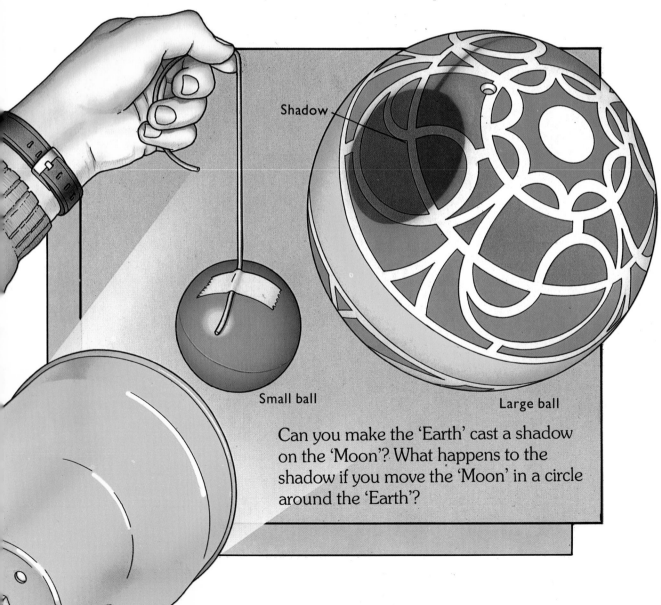

Shadow

Small ball

Large ball

Can you make the 'Earth' cast a shadow on the 'Moon'? What happens to the shadow if you move the 'Moon' in a circle around the 'Earth'?

▲ This photograph shows what happens when the Moon passes in front of the Sun. It stops Sunlight from reaching the Earth and makes some places on Earth dark during the daytime. This is called a Solar eclipse – 'Solar' means to do with the Sun.

For a Solar eclipse to happen, the Moon, the Sun and the Earth all have to be in a straight line. This does not happen very often.

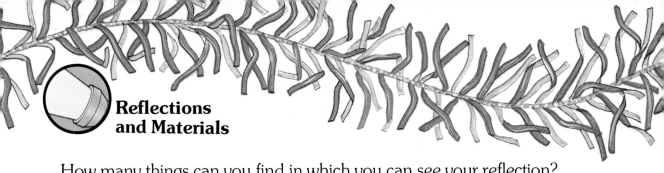

Reflections and Materials

How many things can you find in which you can see your reflection? Look for your reflection out of doors in shop windows, car bonnets and buildings. Can you see your reflection in water? What happens to your reflection if the water is moving?

In a dark room, shine a torch on to different materials such as tin foil, brick, wood, plastic, cloth and metal. Which materials give the best reflections?

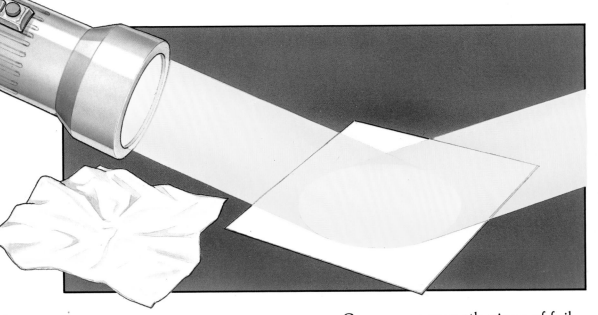

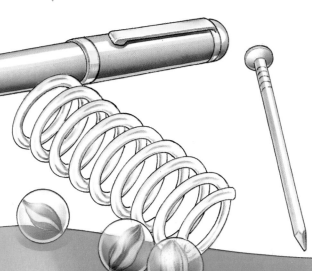

Compare a smooth piece of foil with a wrinkled piece of foil. Can you see your face in both pieces of foil?

Make a collection of shiny materials. You could sort your collection into groups according to the materials the objects are made of – metal or non-metal for example.

67

Mirror, Mirror

Smooth, shiny surfaces produce the best reflections. This is why mirrors are made of a flat sheet of glass with a thin layer of shiny metal, such as silver or aluminium behind the glass.

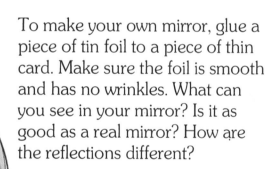

To make your own mirror, glue a piece of tin foil to a piece of thin card. Make sure the foil is smooth and has no wrinkles. What can you see in your mirror? Is it as good as a real mirror? How are the reflections different?

How many different mirrors can you find at home, at school, along the street or in the shops? What shapes and sizes are they? How are they used?

▶ Dancers and actors would find it difficult to put on their make-up properly without a mirror.

Look in the Mirror

Look at your reflection in a mirror. Does your reflection do what you do?
Touch your right ear. Which ear does your reflection touch?

Your reflection seems to be touching its left ear. The reflection is the wrong way round and does not show you as other people see you.

A reflection does not come from the surface of a mirror. It seems to be behind the mirror. Try measuring the distance between you and the mirror. You will find that your reflection appears to be the same distance behind the mirror as you are in front of it.

Mirror Maze

To find out more about the reflections in mirrors, play this game with your friends.

1. Draw a large star shape on a piece of paper.
2. Draw a second star a few millimetres outside the first one.
3. Use some books to prop a large mirror upright on a table. Or ask a friend to hold the mirror for you.
4. Hold a large book in front of your star maze so you can see the reflection but not the actual drawing.
5. Now, looking only in the mirror, try to draw around the maze without touching either of the lines.
6. How fast can you do this? Can your friends beat your fastest time? If they touch the lines, they must start again.

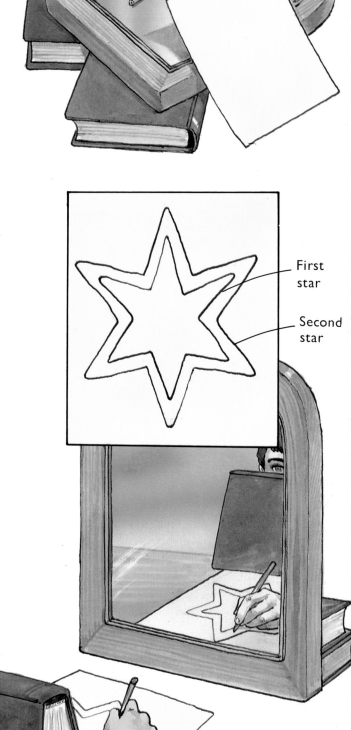

First star

Second star

 **Mirror Writing**

Write your name in big letters on a piece of paper. Hold the paper in front of a mirror. Can you read your name? What has happened to the letters?

Many ambulances have the word 'AMBULANCE' written back to front on the outside of the vehicle. This is so that other drivers see the word the right way round when they look in their rear-view mirrors. It helps drivers to spot an ambulance coming up behind them.

Hold up this book behind your head and look at the picture below in a mirror. In your mirror, is the word the right way round?

Secret Mirror Code

You can use a mirror to invent your own secret code. Only someone with a mirror will be able to read your messages.

The trick is to write your messages while looking only in the mirror. Write each letter slowly so it looks correct in the mirror. Don't look down at the piece of paper.

When you have finished your message, it will look strange because the letters are back to front. Some of the letters will not change. Which ones are they?

Matching Quiz

Some things can be divided by an imaginary line into two parts that look exactly the same. These things are called symmetrical objects. You can find out if something is symmetrical by putting a mirror along the dividing line. If the object looks the same in the mirror, it has a kind of symmetry.

See if you can guess which of the objects below are symmetrical. Test them by holding a mirror against each picture.

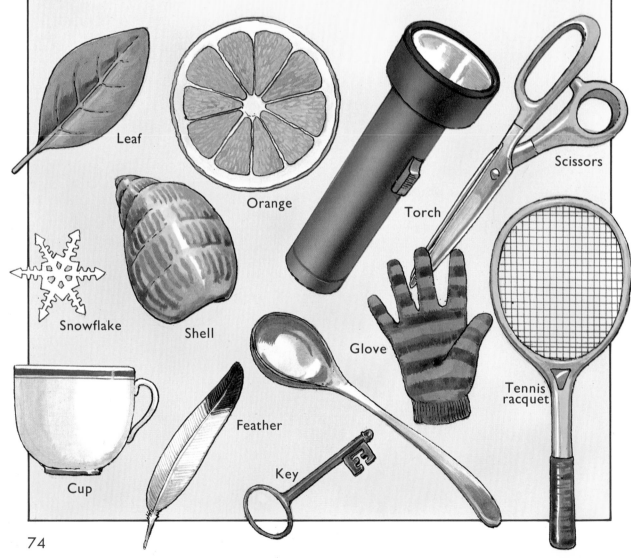

Leaf

Orange

Torch

Scissors

Snowflake

Shell

Glove

Tennis racquet

Cup

Feather

Key

74

Funny Faces

Is your face symmetrical? Find a photograph of yourself which shows your whole face from the front. Hold a mirror down the middle of the photograph. Look at both sides of your face. Does your face look strange?

Mirror Painting

To make a symmetrical painting, **you will need:** newspaper, plain paper, poster paints, jar of water, paintbrush, apron.

1. Put on the apron and lay some newspaper on a table or on the floor so you won't make a mess.
2. Mix up several different colours with the poster paints. Make each colour fairly thick.
3. Use the brush to drop or brush paint on to one side of the paper.
4. Fold the paper over and press down to smooth out the paint.

What happens

When you open out the paper, you will have a painting that is the same on both sides, just as if you were looking in a mirror.

BOUNCING LIGHT

Reflections are caused by light bouncing off things. When this light is reflected into our eyes, we are able to see things.

Catch the Light

Use a small mirror to reflect a spot of light from the Sun or a lamp on to a wall. If you turn the mirror a little, the light spot will move too. Ask a friend to make another light spot on the same wall. Can your friend touch your light spot with the one they have made?

 **Bouncing Back**

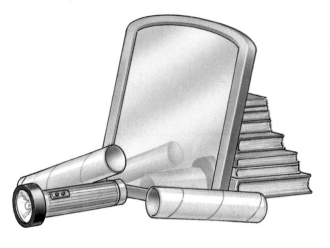

When light hits a smooth surface, it always bounces back at a matching angle. To see how this works, try this test.

You will need: a large mirror, two cardboard tubes, a torch, some books.

1. Use the books to prop the mirror upright.
2. Hold one tube at an angle with the end touching the mirror.
3. Ask a friend to hold the second tube at a matching angle.

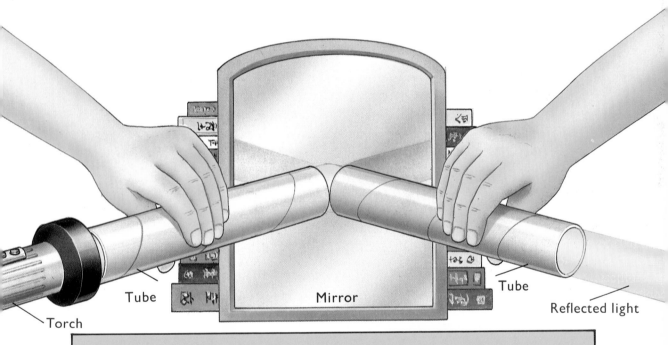

Torch

Tube

Mirror

Tube

Reflected light

What happens

When the tubes are at the correct angle, the light will bounce off the mirror and down to the end of the second tube. If your friend holds their hand at the end of the tube, they will see a circle of reflected light.

On a rough surface, light is not reflected like this. It is scattered back in several different directions.

▲ These rows of mirrors reflect the Sun's rays on to the tower, which is a Solar heat collector. This concentrates a lot of the Sun's energy in one place. The mirrors turn to follow the path of the Sun as it moves across the sky. Solar power is used to generate electricity, to heat and cool buildings and to power small objects such as watches and calculators. Using energy from the Sun does not use up any of the Earth's resources or cause pollution.

 **See-through Brick**

Can you make a light go through a brick?

You will need: a brick, a torch, a piece of cardboard, four small mirrors, modelling clay, scissors.

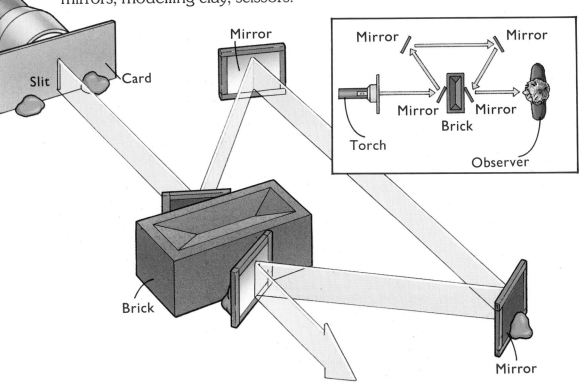

1. Cut a narrow slit about six centimetres deep in the middle of one edge of the piece of cardboard.
2. Use some modelling clay to prop the cardboard upright.
3. Place the brick a little way in front of the card.
4. Use the modelling clay to fix the mirrors to match those in the picture.
5. Shine the torch through the slit.

What happens

The light bounces from one mirror to another and looks as if it is coming straight through the brick.

Multiplying Mirrors

When two mirrors are held together at an angle, the light bounces to and fro between the mirrors. This means you can see more than one reflection of an object.

Tape two mirrors together along one of the long sides. Use some modelling clay to stand the mirrors upright at a wide angle. Put a small object in front of the mirrors. How many reflections can you see?

Now move the mirrors closer together. Count how many reflections of the object you can see now.

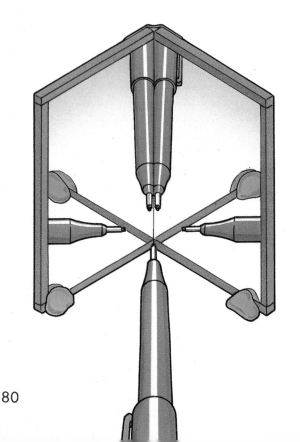

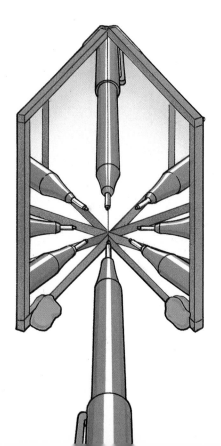

Your Other Face

You can use two mirrors to see yourself as other people see you. To see how this works, you need to make one side of your face look different from the other side. You could use face paints to do this.

Look in one mirror and remember where the painted side of your face appears on your reflection. Then hold two mirrors facing each other at an angle. Move the mirrors until you can see your whole face at the point where the two mirrors join. The painted side of your face will now be on the other side of your reflection.

What happens
With the mirrors at an angle, the reflection of the left side of your face bounces across to the right hand mirror. And the reflection of the right side of your face bounces across to the left hand mirror. When other people look straight at you, they see your face this way round.

How Many Reflections?

Hold a small mirror facing a large mirror so the small mirror is just in front of your nose. As you look over the top of the small mirror, you will be able to see lots and lots of reflections stretching away into the distance. How many reflections can you see? Are all the reflections the same size?

Make a Periscope

Have you ever had your view blocked by a crowd of people? By making a periscope you will be able to see over their heads so you won't miss anything. You can also use a periscope to look round a corner or over a wall without being seen.

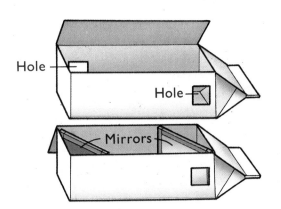

Hole

Hole

Mirrors

You will need: a large empty milk or juice carton, two small mirrors, sticky tape, scissors.

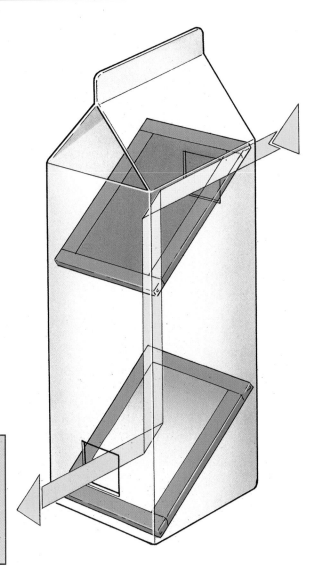

1. On one side of the carton, cut three of the edges to make a lid you can lift up.
2. Cut two holes in opposite sides of the carton, to match the picture.
3. Tape the two mirrors inside the carton. The mirrors should be facing each other at the same angle.
4. Tape down the lid.
5. Hold the periscope upright and look into the bottom mirror.

What happens
The light bounces from one mirror to the other so you can see over people's heads or round corners.

Using periscopes, even people at the back of a large crowd can see what is happening at the front.

Make a Kaleidoscope

The word 'kaleidoscope' means 'beautiful form to look at'. If you make a kaleidoscope, you will be able to see lots of beautiful symmetrical patterns.

You will need: stiff cardboard, a pencil, scissors, black paper or a thick black felt pen, tin foil, glue, clear plastic, tracing paper, sticky tape, small coloured shapes or beads.

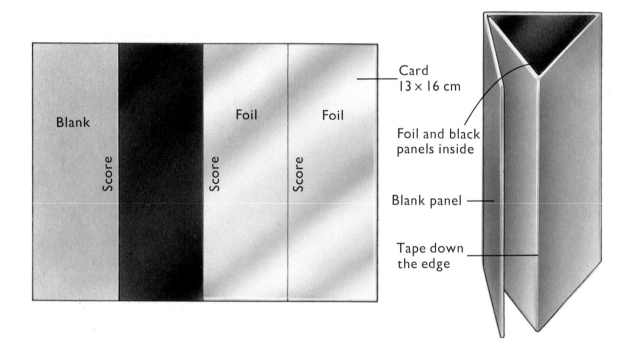

1. Cut out a piece of cardboard about 13 centimetres by 16 centimetres.
2. With the pencil, divide the card into four equal strips. Each strip should be four centimetres wide.
3. Ask an adult to help you score the lines so the card is easier to fold.

4. Stick foil over two of the panels. Make sure it is as smooth as possible.
5. Stick black paper over the third panel or colour it black.
6. Leave the fourth panel blank.
7. Fold the card to make a triangular shape and tape the side to hold it in place.

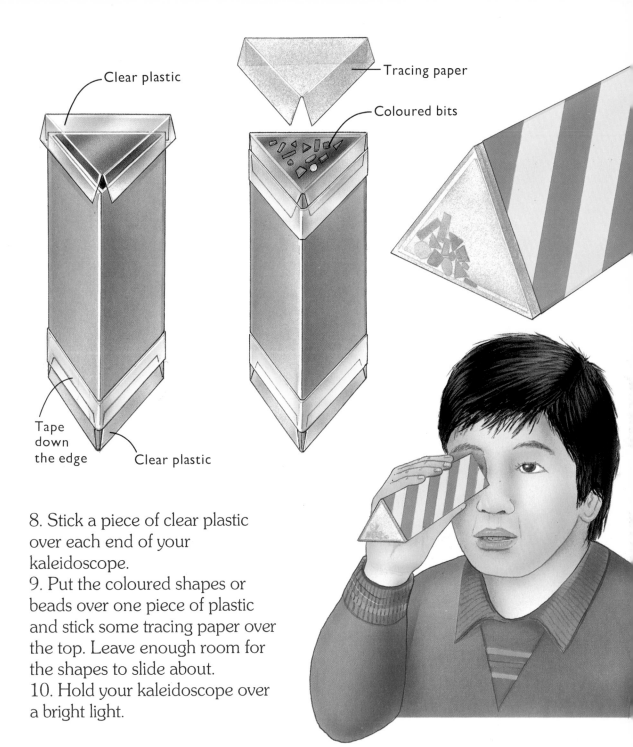

Clear plastic

Tracing paper

Coloured bits

Tape down the edge

Clear plastic

8. Stick a piece of clear plastic over each end of your kaleidoscope.

9. Put the coloured shapes or beads over one piece of plastic and stick some tracing paper over the top. Leave enough room for the shapes to slide about.

10. Hold your kaleidoscope over a bright light.

What happens
The light bounces to and fro between the foil mirrors. The reflections of the coloured shapes or beads make interesting patterns. To change the pattern, shake your kaleidoscope so the shapes or beads move into new positions.

CURVED MIRRORS

Curved mirrors change the size and shape of things reflected in them. Look at your reflection in the curved side of a shiny tin or a saucepan. What do you look like?

Now try a spoon. The back of a spoon curves outwards. This sort of curved mirror makes you look smaller.

What happens to your reflection in the front of a spoon?

▶ The surfaces of these curved mirrors curve both inwards and outwards. Look what it does to these reflections!

TRUE OR FALSE?

1 This book is opaque.

2 If an object is near to a source of light, it casts a small shadow.

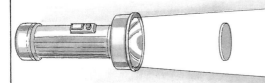

3 Winter shadows are shorter than summer shadows.

4 The Moon does not produce any light of its own.

5 In the front of a spoon, a reflection looks upside down.

6 You can use a periscope to see through a wall.

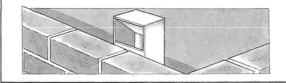

Answers

1 True. You cannot see through the book because it does not allow light to pass through it.

2 False. The object blocks out a lot of light and casts a big shadow.

3 False. In winter, the Sun is low in the sky, so shadows are longer than in summer.

4 True. The Moon shines only because it reflects light from the Sun.

5 True. The way the light is reflected from the curved surface makes the reflection appear upside down.

6 False. Periscopes allow you to see over the top of a wall or round a corner, but not through solid materials.

Machines and Movement

How is your arm like a lever? How does a gymnast keep her balance on a beam? How is a mobile like a see-saw? How do pulleys help us to lift heavy weights? What do gear wheels do? How do forces called friction and gravity affect movement on Earth and in space? How can you use an elastic band to make a weighing machine?

This section will help you to discover the answers to these questions and has lots of ideas for ways to investigate machines and movement.

MACHINES AND MOVEMENT

In this section, you can discover how machines make our lives easier and how forces such as friction and gravity affect movement.

The section is divided into eight different topics. Look out for the big headings with a circle at each end – like the one at the top of this page. These headings tell you where a new topic starts.

Pages 92–99

What is a Machine?

Simple machines; levers; balancing; mobiles.

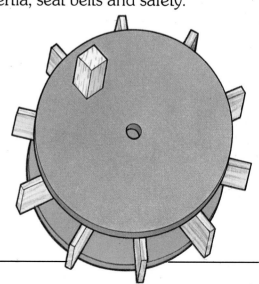

Pages 108–109

Stop and Go

Inertia; seat belts and safety.

Pages 100–107

Wheels go Round

Shapes of wheels; axles; pulleys; gear wheels.

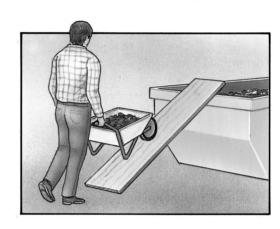

Sticking and Slipping

Friction; brakes; ball bearings; hovercraft.

Slopes and Screws

Angle of slopes; Archimedes screw; wedges.

Stretch and Twist

Elastic materials; spring balances; bouncing.

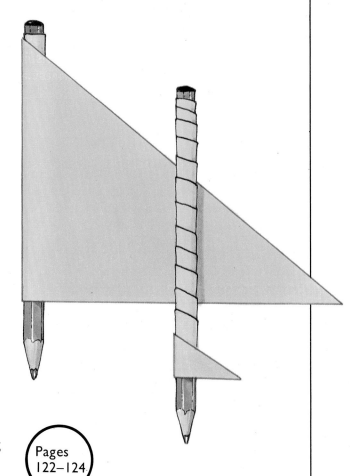

The Pull of the Earth

Gravity and weight.

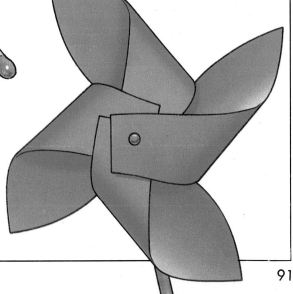

Energy for Machines

Fuel; electricity; wind and water power.

 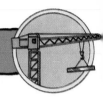

Look at the objects along the bottom of these two pages. Did you know that they are all simple machines? You probably think of machines as big, noisy, complicated things such as lawnmowers, washing machines or robots. But a machine is any device that makes work easier. A machine usually involves movement.

Scissors make it easier to cut things.
A bicycle makes it easier to go fast.
A screw helps to hold pieces of wood together.
A spade makes it easier to dig the garden.
A crane makes it easier to lift heavy weights.

Lever

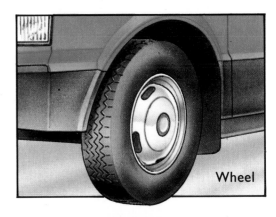

Wheel

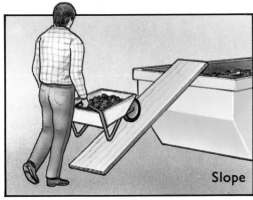

Slope

Wedge

There are five very simple machines that are the basis of all the other machines we use. They are:

the lever
the wheel
the slope
the wedge
the screw

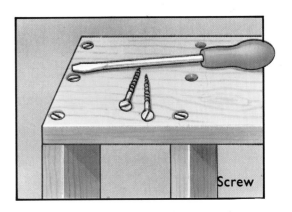

Screw

Look out for these machines as you read this book. Try making a list of all the machines in your home or school. Which room has the most machines?

Lifting with Levers

A lever is a bar that swings, or pivots on a fixed point called a fulcrum. A lever makes it easier to lift heavy things. Your arm is a kind of lever. So are scissors, spades, pliers, tweezers, brooms, wheelbarrows and see-saws. If you push one end of a lever down, the other end moves up.

Make a lever by balancing a plank of wood over a small block of wood. The block is the fulcrum. Try lifting a brick with your lever. Is it easier to lift the brick if the fulcrum is nearer to the brick or farther away?

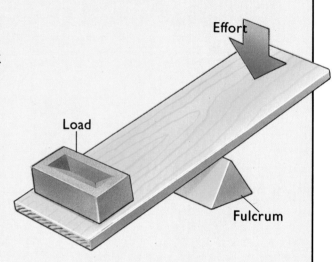

There are three kinds of lever. Each one has the pushing force (the effort), the pivot (fulcrum) and the weight (the load) in different places. This allows each of them to do a different job.

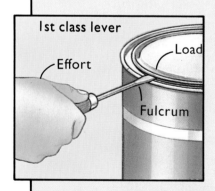

1st class lever

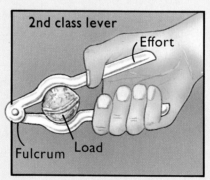

2nd class lever

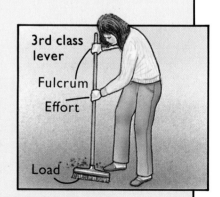

3rd class lever

A first class lever has the fulcrum between the effort and the load. A second class lever has the load between the effort and the fulcrum. A third class lever has the effort between the fulcrum and the load.

94

▲ In this picture, the tennis player's arm is working as a third class lever. The effort is the muscles of the upper arm, which are in between the fulcrum (the shoulder) and the load (the ball hitting the racquet).

Balancing

How good are you at balancing?
Put a ball on the floor near a wall.
Stand with your heels right up
against the wall. Now try to pick
up the ball without moving your
feet.

It's impossible! When you bend over, your balancing point moves
fowards. To keep your balance, you have to move your feet forwards
too. The balancing point of an object is called its centre of gravity .

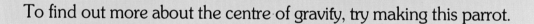

Perching Parrot

To find out more about the centre of gravify, try making this parrot.

You will need: cardboard, modelling clay, scissors, coloured pencils,
a drawing pencil.

1. Draw a parrot shape on the cardboard. Make sure it has a long tail
which curves under the body, like the one in the picture.
2. Colour in your parrot and cut it out.
3. Put a lump of modelling clay on the end of the tail.
4. Balance your parrot on the end of your finger or on a pencil perch. It
should rock to and fro on its perch. You may have to add or take away
some clay to get the balance just right.

▲ On the balance beam, a gymnast has to keep her centre of gravity right in the middle of her body. Otherwise she will fall off the beam.

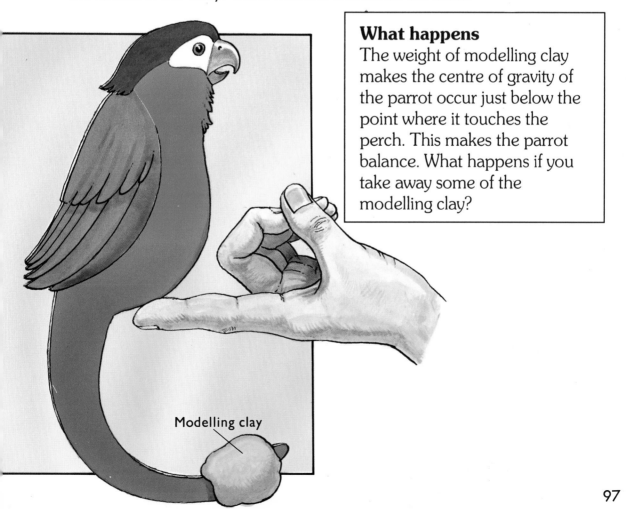

Modelling clay

What happens
The weight of modelling clay makes the centre of gravity of the parrot occur just below the point where it touches the perch. This makes the parrot balance. What happens if you take away some of the modelling clay?

Make a Mobile

A mobile is a balancing act you can make yourself. Moving air pushes it around.

You will need: cardboard, straws, a hole punch, thread, scissors.

1. Draw some shapes on the cardboard and colour them in. Cut out the shapes.
2. Use the hole punch to make a hole in each shape.
3. Cut a small slit in both ends of each straw. It's easier to do this if you flatten the straw before you cut it.
4. Use the thread to tie one shape to each end of one straw.
5. Find the point where the straw hangs level (the balancing point) and tie a thread around the straw at this point.
6. Tie the other end of the thread to one end of a second straw.
7. Tie a shape to the other end of the second straw so that the second straw balances.
8. Keep adding more shapes until your mobile has four layers, which all balance.
9. Hang up your mobile and watch it move. How is a mobile like a see-saw?

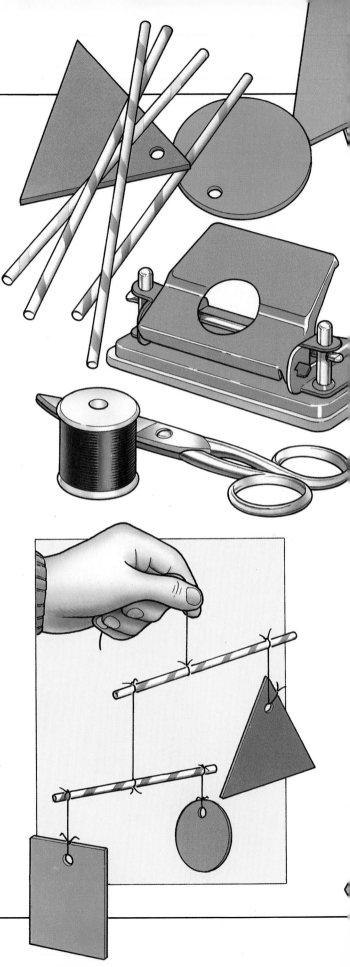

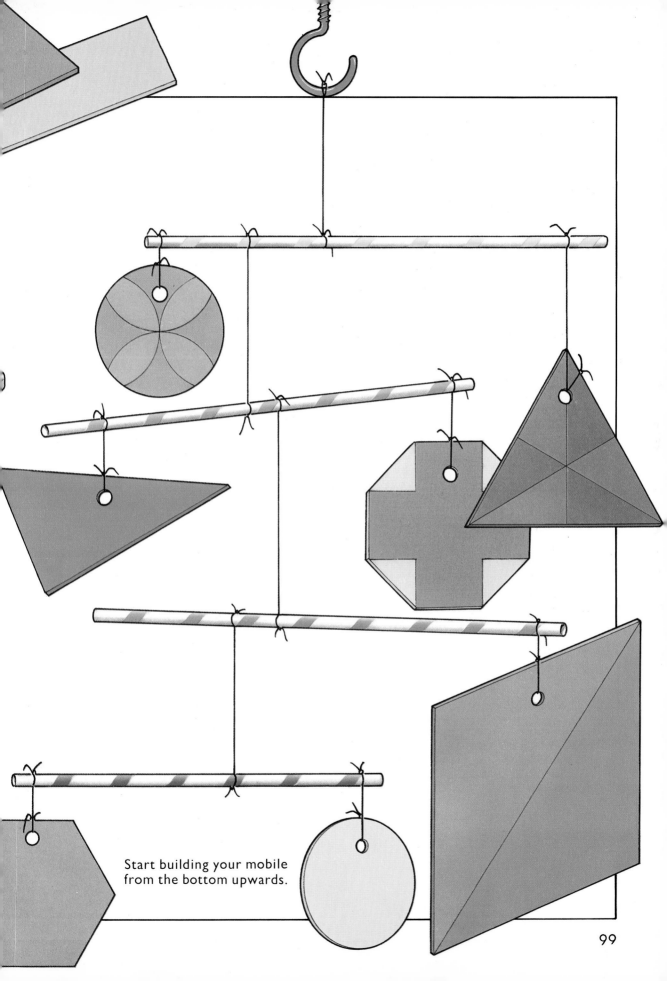

Start building your mobile from the bottom upwards.

WHEELS GO ROUND

Wheels help us to move things along the ground. They are also used to make pots and spin wool. What else are wheels used for?

 Wheels and Axles

A wheel on its own is not much use. It needs something to turn on. This is called an axle. Use straws, pencils or thin dowel as axles and cut out wheels from thin card or balsa wood. Use modelling clay to fix the axles to the wheels. You can make the axle and the wheel turn together. Or you can leave the wheel free to turn while the axle stays still.

What happens if the axle is not in the middle of the wheel? Try making different shaped wheels. Which shape turns round most easily?

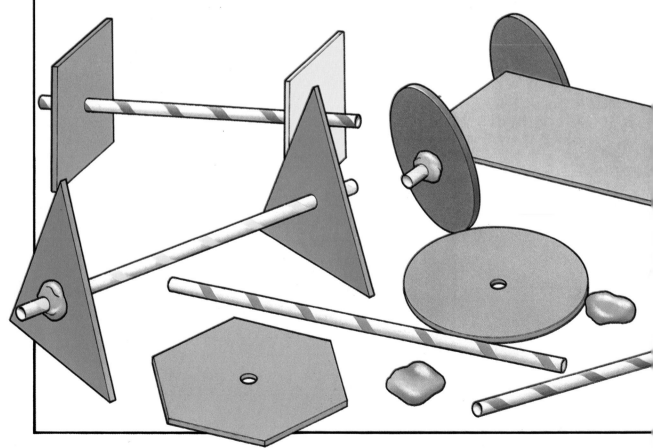

▲ The wheel is one of the most important inventions ever made. No one knows who invented the wheel but it has been used for thousands of years. This mosaic of a Sumerian cart is nearly 4500 years old.

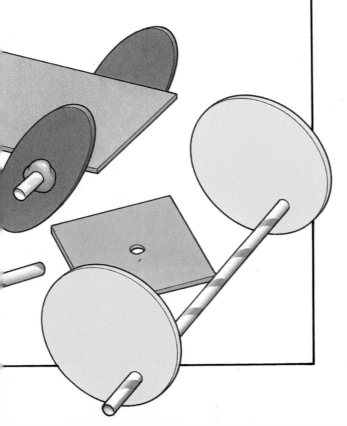

Make a Land Yacht

1. Use the scissors to cut two holes near the bottom of one of the long sides of the box. Cut two matching holes on the other side.
2. Push the axles through the holes to match the picture.
3. Use the glue or modelling clay to fix the wheels to the axles.

You will need:

A small box, 3 or 4 wheels made from card, wood or cotton reels, 2 axles made from straws or dowel, a sail made from paper or cloth and straws or dowel, a mast made from a straw or a garden cane, scissors, glue, modelling clay, cotton thread.

4. Tie the sail to the mast using the thread.
5. Cut slots in the box to match the picture. Push the mast through the slots and use modelling clay to stand the sail up inside the box.
6. Take your land yacht to a place with a strong wind or roll it down a steep slope. How fast does it move?

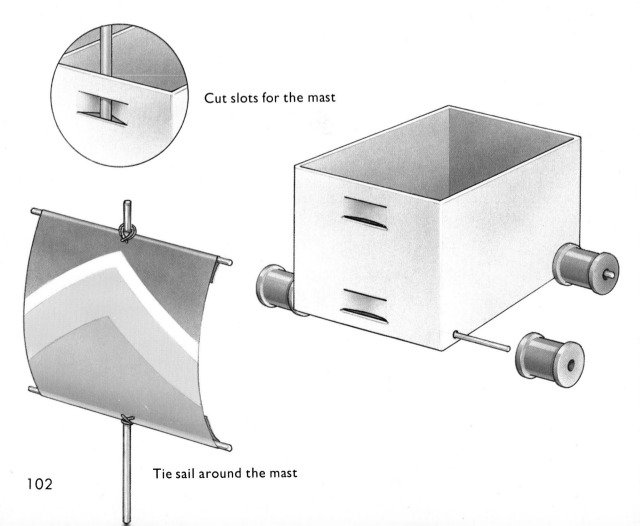

Cut slots for the mast

Tie sail around the mast

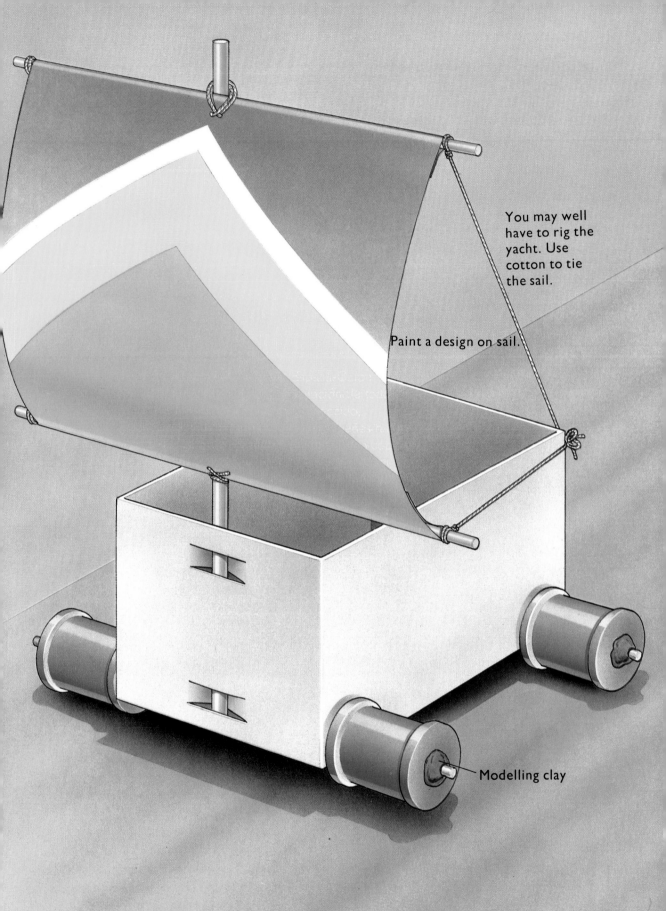

You may well have to rig the yacht. Use cotton to tie the sail.

Paint a design on sail.

Modelling clay

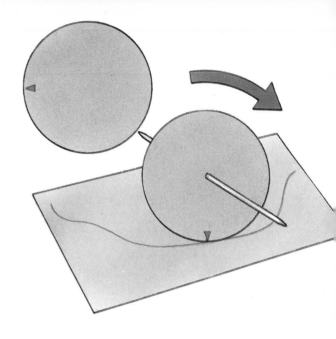

Wheels for Measuring

Wheels can be used for measuring distances. Make a measuring wheel yourself. Cut out a circle of card and push a cocktail stick through the middle. Make a mark on the edge of the wheel. Lay your wheel on a piece of paper and use the mark to help you measure the distance the wheel takes to turn round once.

How far do you go for one turn of your bicycle wheel? Ask a friend to help you measure the distance.

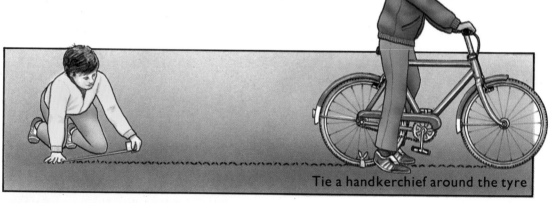

Tie a handkerchief around the tyre

◀ Trains run on wheels with a sloping edge, like an ice-cream cone. This shape helps the train to stay on the track. These children are experimenting with different shaped wheels to see which ones are best at staying on the track.

Real train wheels have a special edge called a flange, which helps to keep the engine and coaches from falling off the track.

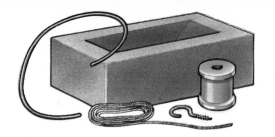

 **Wheels for Lifting**

A wheel with a groove for carrying a rope is called a pulley. By pulling down on the rope, we can lift heavy things up. Look out for pulleys in cranes, in lifts, on sailing ships and on some washing lines.

You will need: A cotton reel, wire, metal hook, string, a weight such as a brick or a heavy book.

1. Ask an adult to help you fix the hook into a wooden beam.
2. Bend the wire through the cotton reel and make a loop above the reel.
3. Hang the reel over the hook.
4. Tie the string around the weight.
5. Leave the weight on the floor and loop the other end of the string around the cotton reel.
6. When you pull down on the free end of the string, the weight will rise up off the ground. This is much easier than lifting the brick with your bare hands.

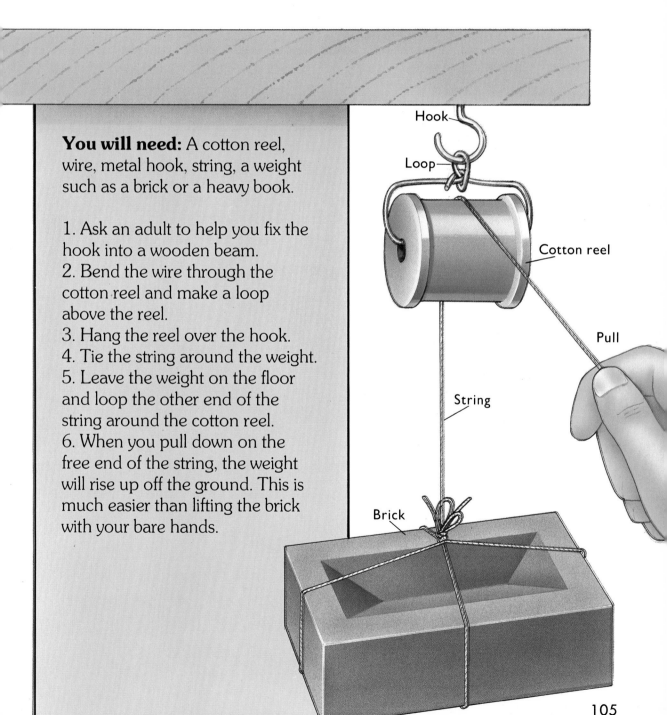

Hook

Loop

Cotton reel

Pull

String

Brick

Wheels with Teeth

A wheel with teeth around the edge is called a gear wheel. To make a gear wheel, cut two circles of card. Make a hole through the middle of both circles. Stick pieces of thin wood on to one piece of card. Arrange them in a wheel shape so the end of the wood sticks out around the edge of the circle. Stick the other circle on top.

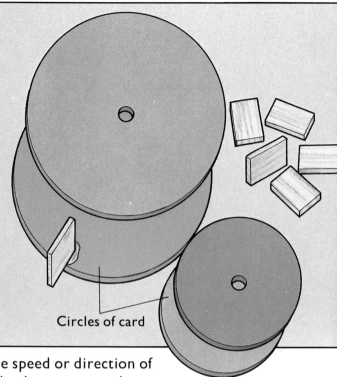

Circles of card

▼ Gear wheels are used to change the speed or direction of movement. Inside a clock, the gear wheels are arranged so they make the big hand and the little hand turn at different speeds.

To start with, make one big wheel and one small wheel. Push a pencil through the middle of each wheel and push the pencil through a large piece of card. Arrange the gear wheels so the teeth link together.

Turn the big wheel once. Which way does the small wheel turn? How many times does the small wheel turn round? Does the small wheel turn faster or slower than the small wheel?

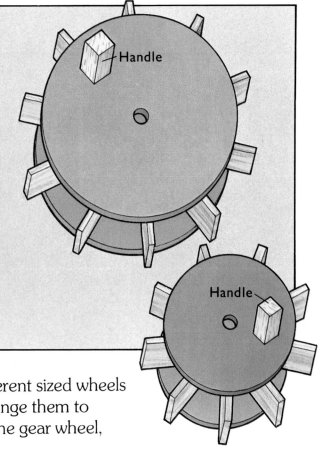

To make a gear machine, make different sized wheels with different numbers of teeth. Arrange them to match the picture. When you turn one gear wheel, what happens to the other wheels?

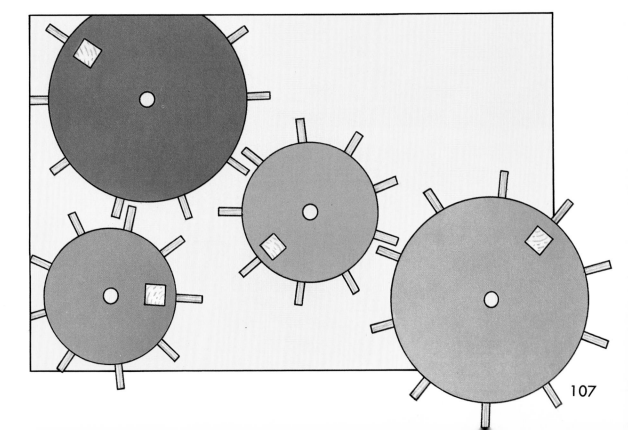

STOP AND GO

Have you ever been in a car that stopped suddenly? The sudden force throws you forwards after the car has stopped. A seat belt keeps you in your seat so you don't hit the seats or the windscreen.

You are thrown forwards because of something called inertia. Inertia is a physical property that keeps moving things moving or stationary things still – unless a strong force acts on them. The word inertia comes from the Latin word for laziness.

Flick the Paper

Put a plastic beaker on a piece of paper. Can you pull the paper out from under the mug without knocking it over?

The trick is to pull the paper out very sharply. The mug will be left behind because the pulling force is not strong enough to overcome its inertia. Can you repeat the trick with a mug full of water?

In a Spin

Find two table tennis balls and make a small hole in each one. Make up some jelly and pour the liquid jelly into one of the balls. Leave the jelly to set hard. Pour water into the other ball. Put tape across the holes.

Now spin each ball in turn on a smooth surface. Stop the ball with your fingers and then let go. What happens?

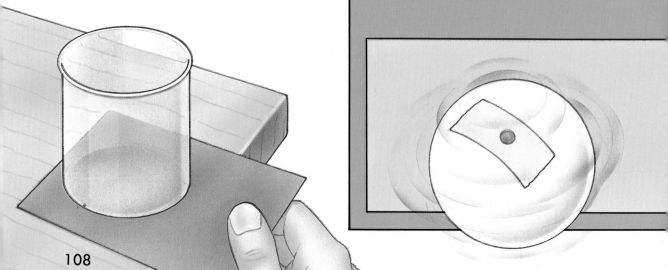

Snapping Strings

Put 500 grammes of small stones or marbles into a small plastic bag. Tie a long piece of thread to the top of the bag and another piece of thread to the bottom of the bag. Rest a stick or broom handle over two chairs and tie the top thread to the stick. Pull the bottom thread sharply. What happens?

Now tie another piece of thread to the bottom of the bag. Pull the bottom thread slowly. What happens this time?

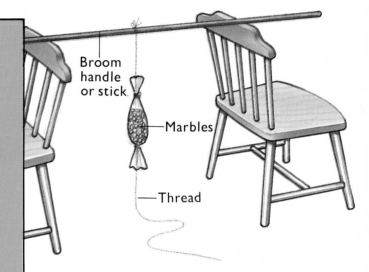

Broom handle or stick

Marbles

Thread

What happens

The water ball will start spinning again when you let go. Inertia keeps the water swirling around inside the ball and this starts the ball spinning again. There is no movement inside the jelly ball. So when you stop it spinning, it stays still. You can use this trick to help you tell the difference between a raw egg and a cooked egg.

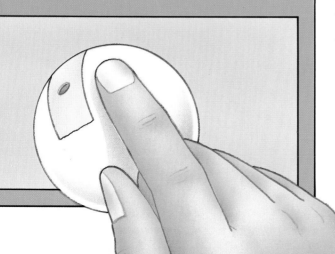

What happens

When you pull the bottom thread sharply, the inertia of the stones stops the pull from reaching the top thread. So the bottom thread snaps. When you pull the bottom thread slowly, the steady pull is a strong enough force to overcome the inertia of the stones. This time, the pull reaches the top thread and it snaps first.

STICKING AND SLIPPING

Rub your hands together very quickly. The heat you feel is caused by a force called friction. Friction tries to stop things sliding past each other and slows things down. Without friction, we would slip over every time we tried to walk.

 Science Friction

To find out more about the friction on different surfaces, try these tests.

You will need: a table, string, scissors, a wooden block, a yoghurt pot, marbles, a hook, different surfaces: carpet tiles, sandpaper, shiny hardboard, newspaper.

1. To protect the table, cover it with an old cloth or blanket.
2. Fit the hook into one side of the wooden block.
3. Tie one end of the string to the yoghurt pot and the other end to the hook.

4. Put each surface on to the table in turn.
5. Put the block on top of the surface.
6. To make the block move, how many marbles do you need to put in the yoghurt pot?

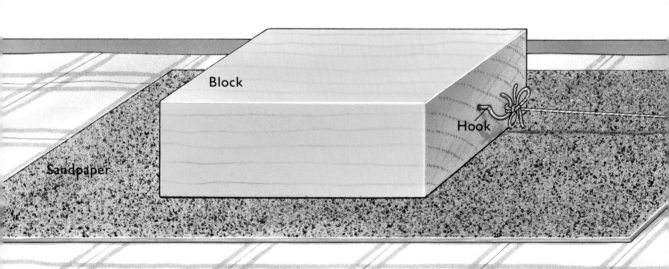

Block

Hook

Sandpaper

▲ Skis are very narrow so that only a small surface comes into contact with the snow. They are also smooth underneath. This reduces the amount of friction between the skis and the snow and helps skiers to slide at high speeds over the snow.

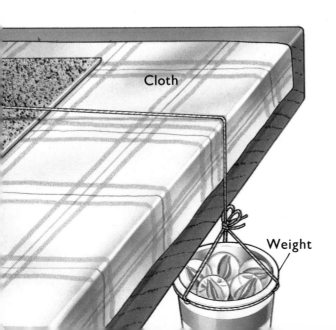

Cloth

Weight

What happens

The rough surfaces cause more friction. You need more marbles in the pot to overcome this friction and make the block move. Which surface causes the most friction?

 **Braking Power**

A lot of friction can sometimes be useful. Bicycle brakes work because of friction. When you squeeze the brakes, rubber or plastic pads press against the wheel rims and stop the wheels turning.

Next time you brake hard, stop and feel the wheel rim. It will be warm because of friction.

Too much Friction

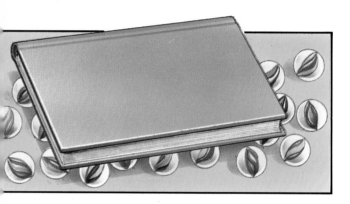

Try pushing a book along the carpet. Friction stops the book sliding along easily. Now put some marbles under the book and push it again. This time it moves easily because the marbles roll and cut down the friction.

Sometimes, friction is a problem. In machines, it makes moving parts get hot and wear out more quickly. It also wastes energy. Ball bearings are used to help the moving parts inside machines spin more easily. A bearing is often made of a ring of smooth, shiny balls which roll around in a groove between the fixed and the moving parts of a machine. This reduces friction.

Ball bearings

 **Make a Hovercraft**

A hovercraft floats above the ground or the water on a cushion of air. This cuts down the amount of friction and helps the hovercraft to move more easily.

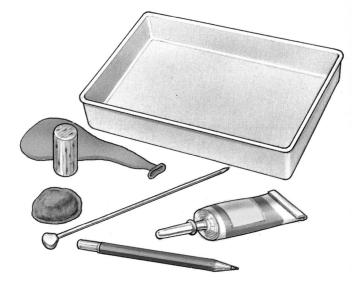

You will need: a balloon, a polystyrene food tray, a small cork, glue, a knitting needle, modelling clay, a pencil.

1. Ask an adult to use the knitting needle to make a hole through the middle of the cork.
2. Use the pencil to make a small hole in the middle of the food tray.
3. Glue the cork to the bottom of the tray so the holes are lined up.
4. Put modelling clay around the cork to stop air escaping.
5. Put the tray on a smooth surface.
6. Blow up the balloon. Hold the end tightly so the air can't get out and fit the nozzle of the balloon over the cork.
7. Give the tray a gentle push and it should glide away.

What happens

The air from the balloon rushes down through the cork and out under the tray. The air lifts the tray a little way off the floor. When you push your hovercraft, it glides along on this layer of air, just like a real hovercraft.

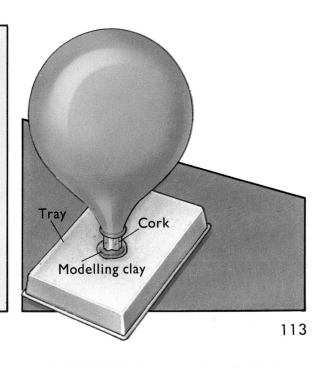

Tray

Cork

Modelling clay

SLOPES AND SCREWS

It is easier to pull a heavy weight up a slope than to lift it straight up. Prove this for yourself. Tie a piece of string around a stone and tie an elastic band to the string. To make a slope, pile up several books and rest a ruler against the books. Use the elastic band to pull the stone up the ruler. How far does the band stretch?

Now take away the ruler and lift the stone straight up from the floor to to the top of the books. Does the elastic band stretch farther this time?

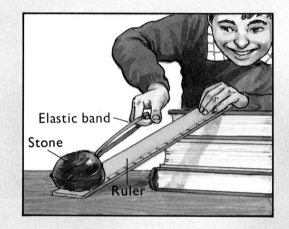

Elastic band

Stone

Ruler

Sliding down Slopes

Tie a piece of string to a heavy object, such as a book or a brick. Pull the string through a bulldog clip. Tie the other end of the string to a handle or fixed bar. Put the bulldog clip at the top of the slope. How long does it take to slide down? Change the angle of the slope. How does this change the speed of the bulldog clip? Try sliding other objects, such as rolls of tape or paper clips, down your slope. How does the size and weight of the object affect its speed down the slope?

Bulldog clip

Rolled-up-Slopes

Screws can be used to lift things, press things or force things apart. A screw holds two pieces of wood together more firmly than a nail.

A screw is really a rolled-up slope. You can check this for yourself. Draw a slope on a piece of paper and cut it out. Then wind the paper around a pencil. Compare this with a real screw.

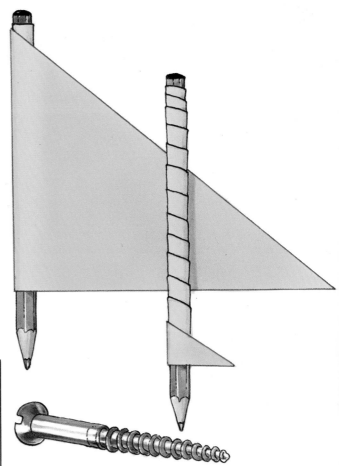

Did you know that a wedge is two slopes joined back-to-back? An axe is a kind of wedge. If you push a wedge into a gap, you force the load past its sloping sides. This makes it easier to force things apart.

This edge of a screw is called a thread.

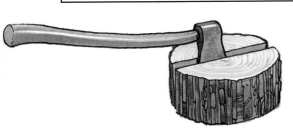

▶ This model of an Archimedes screw is being used to lift grain up out of a pit into a hopper. This machine was invented thousands of years ago by the Greek scientist Archimedes. In Egypt, it is still used to lift water for irrigation.

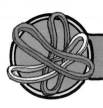

STRETCH AND TWIST

Pull some of the skin on your arm. How far will your skin stretch? What happens when you let go? Materials that stretch but go back to their original shape are called elastic materials.

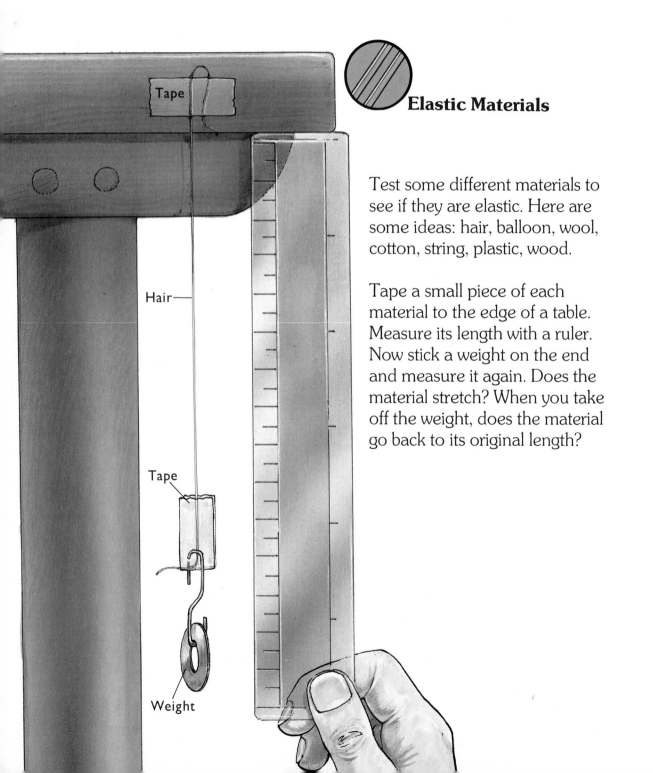

Elastic Materials

Test some different materials to see if they are elastic. Here are some ideas: hair, balloon, wool, cotton, string, plastic, wood.

Tape a small piece of each material to the edge of a table. Measure its length with a ruler. Now stick a weight on the end and measure it again. Does the material stretch? When you take off the weight, does the material go back to its original length?

Tape

Hair

Tape

Weight

Make a Weighing Machine

Rubber is an elastic material. You can use an elastic band to make a weighing machine.

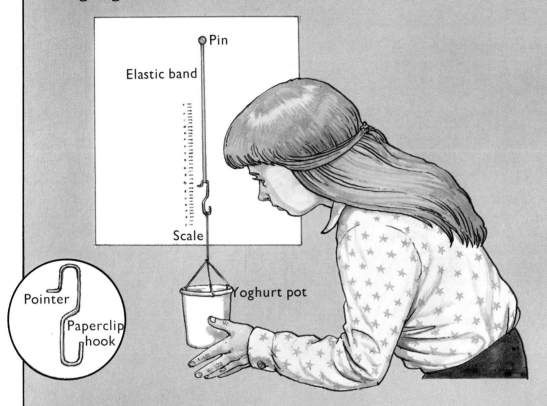

Pin

Elastic band

Scale

Yoghurt pot

Pointer

Paperclip hook

You will need: A large piece of cardboard, a pen, a paperclip, strong thread, a yoghurt pot, an elastic band, a strong pin or nail, a ruler.

1. Stick the pin or nail into the card and hang the elastic band from the pin or nail.

2. Open out the paperclip to make a hook shape at one end and a pointer at the other end.

3. Tie one end of the thread or string around the rim of the pot and tie the other end to the paper clip.

4. Put a known weight in the pot and mark the position of the pointer.

5. Put more known weights in the pot, one at a time, until you have made a scale on the cardboard.

6. Use your weighing machine to weigh different objects such as marbles, pencils, stones and paper clips. Make a chart of your results.

 **Make a Cotton Reel Tank**

This tank rolls along using the energy from a twisted elastic band.

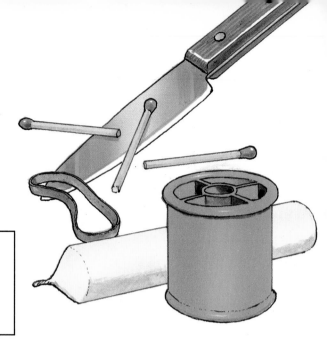

You will need: A cotton reel, a small elastic band, three matchsticks, a candle, a ruler, a knife.

Ask an adult to help you with the first three steps.

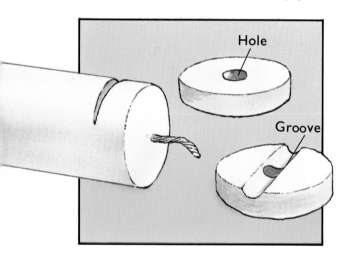

Hole

Groove

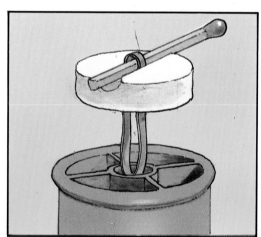

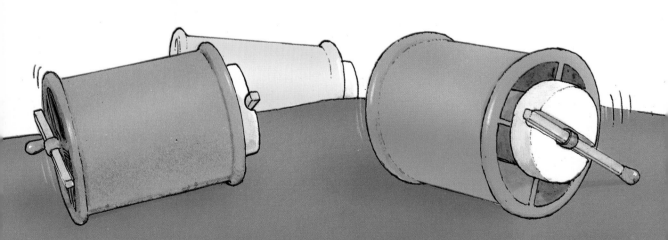

1. Cut a thin slice of wax from the candle.
2. Use the knife to make a hole in the middle of the slice.
3. Make a groove in one side of the slice straight across the middle.
4. Push the elastic band through the hole in the slice and put a matchstick through the band. Pull the band so the matchstick is held in the groove.
5. Pull the other end of the band through the hole in the middle of the cotton reel.
6. Push half a matchstick through the band to hold it in place.
7. Push another matchstick into one of the holes through the reel. This will stop the half matchstick from turning round.
8. To twist the elastic band, turn the matchstick in the groove around several times.
9. When you put your tank on the floor or on a table, the band will slowly unwind and push the tank along.
10. You could have a tank race with your friends.

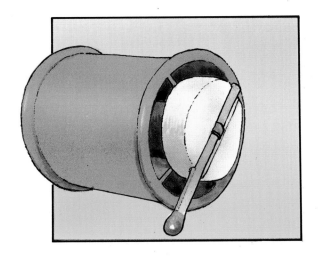

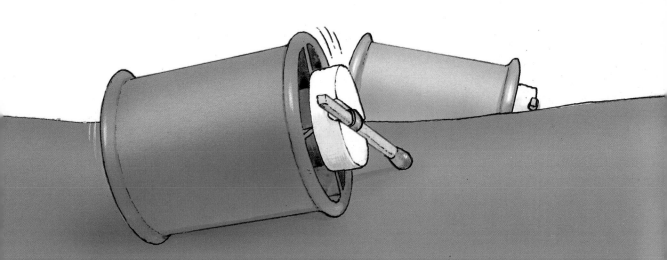

How high can you make a rubber ball bounce? Draw a scale on a large piece of paper. Drop a ball from different heights and ask a friend to mark how high the ball bounces each time.

Drop several different balls from the same height. Which one bounces the highest? What is this ball made from?

Which sort of surface is best for bouncing? Try grass, soil, wood, sand, cement and carpet.

Bouncing Game

Half fill a bucket with sand. Stand three metres away from the bucket. See if you and your friends can get the ball into the bucket with just one bounce. Draw a picture of the path of the bounce. If you stand farther way from the bucket, does the path of the bounce change?

◄ When a ball hits the ground the bottom part of it is squashed and pushed upwards. The ball then springs back into shape, which pushes it up into the air. In the photograph, you can see that the second bounce is lower than the first one.

THE PULL OF THE EARTH

If you throw a ball up in the air, it falls back down to the ground. This happens because of a force called gravity, which pulls things down to the ground. The Earth is so big that the pull of its gravity is very strong. It keeps everything on the Earth. We rely on gravity to pour drinks, post letters or drill holes. Without gravity, everything on Earth would fly off into space.

These astronauts are learning to cope with the 'weightless' feeling they will experience out in Space. On Earth, we have weight because gravity pulls us down to the ground.

Falling Forces

To see how gravity affects falling objects, try these tests.

You will need: newspaper, large sheets of paper, a straw or eyedropper, tape, thin paint or ink.

1. Put lots of newspaper on the floor.
2. Tape a sheet of paper on top of the newspaper.
3. Pick up some of the thin paint or ink with the straw or eyedropper.
4. Drop the paint or ink from a height of 10 centimetres, 30 centimetres, 50 centimetres and 100 centimetres.
5. Before you let each drop fall, guess the size of the blob it will make on the paper.
6. What happens if you drop thicker paint or ink from the same heights?

To make a straw dropper

Hold your finger over the end of a straw. Dip it into the paint or ink. The paint or ink will not fall out until you take your finger off the end of the straw.

What happens

When the paint or ink drops fall from a greater height, gravity makes them fall faster. They are travelling at a faster speed when they hit the ground, so they make bigger marks on the paper.

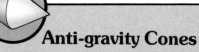

Anti-gravity Cones

The cones in this investigation seem to roll uphill, against the force of gravity. How is this possible?

1. Cut two pieces of cardboard to match the shape in the picture.
2. Tape the two shortest sides of the card together.
3. Hold the paper by one of the corners on the long side. Make a cone shape by curling the other corner on the long side around your hand. Ask a friend to help you tape the paper to hold it in place.
4. Use scissors to trim the point off the open end of the cone to make a circle.
5. Make another cone exactly the same size and shape. Tape the open ends of the cones together to match the picture.
6. Put the paper cones at the bottom of the hill and watch them climb upwards.

You will need:

Cardboard, plain paper about 20 centimetres by 13 centimetres, a pencil, a ruler, scissors, tape.

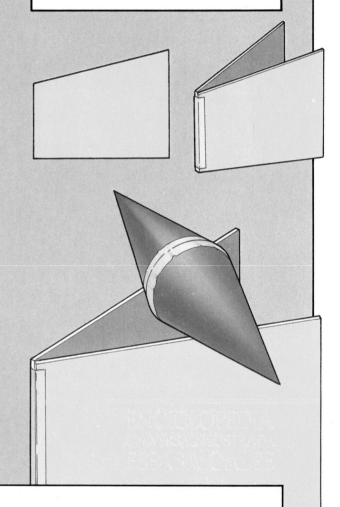

What happens

The middle part of the cones really goes downhill. So the cones are not going against the force of gravity. You can prove this by measuring the distance from the middle of the cones to the ground when they are at the top of the hill. At this point, the cones will be lower down than at the bottom of the hill.

Machines need energy to make them work. This power can come from petrol, electricity and the pushing force of water or the wind. Can you think of any other sources of energy for machines?

Make a Windmill

You will need:

A piece of coloured paper about 15 centimetres square, scissors, a pin, a bead, a stick.

1. Cut lines in the piece of paper to match the picture.
2. Fold in the pieces marked with a cross.
3. Push the pin through the middle of the folded pieces.
4. Thread a bead on to the back of the pin.
5. Ask an adult to help you push the pin into a stick.
6. On a windy day, put the windmill outside and see how fast it turns round.

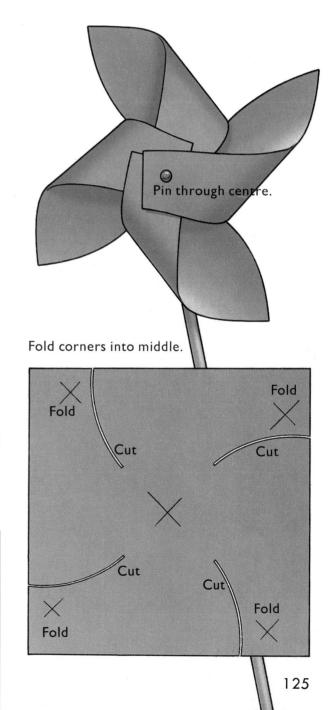

Pin through centre.

Fold corners into middle.

Fold

Fold

Cut

Cut

Fold

Cut

Cut

Fold

Windmills can be used to grind flour or raise water from a well. Nowadays, special windmills are used to make electricity. This does not pollute the environment, but it is only possible in places where there are a lot of strong winds.

125

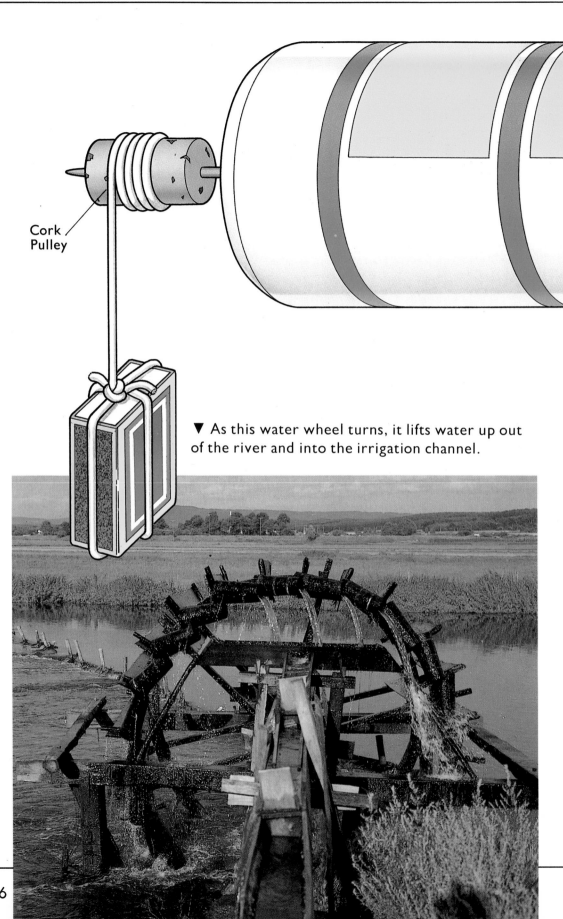

Cork
Pulley

▼ As this water wheel turns, it lifts water up out of the river and into the irrigation channel.

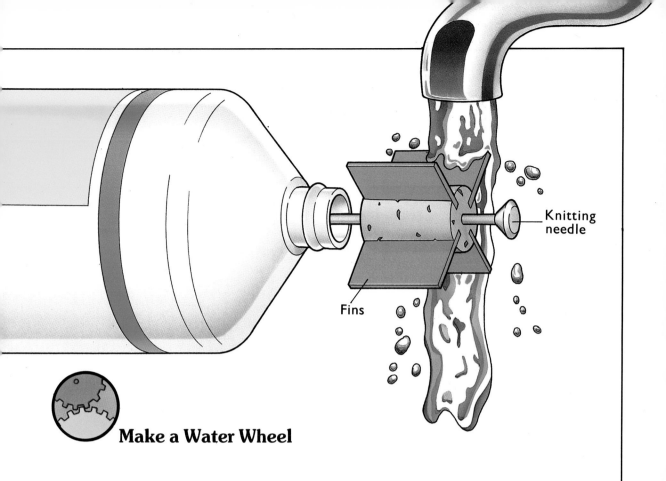

Knitting
needle

Fins

Make a Water Wheel

You will need: A plastic bottle, two corks, small pieces of plastic or thin balsa wood, a knitting needle, scissors, thread, a matchbox.

1. Cut four plastic or wooden fins.
2. Ask an adult to make four slits in the sides of the cork and one hole through the middle of the cork.
3. Push the fins into the slits in the cork.
4. Make a hole in the bottom of the plastic bottle.
5. Push the knitting needle through the cork with the fins, into the bottle and out through the hole in the bottom.
6. Then push the point of the knitting needle into the other cork. The needle should not be able to turn round inside either cork.
7. Hold the bottle, put your water wheel under a tap and watch it turn round.
8. Tie a long thread with a matchbox on the end to the second cork. As the water wheel turns, it will lift up the matchbox. Can you make your water wheel work any other machines?

TRUE OR FALSE?

1 Scissors and see-saws are both kinds of lever.

2 Smooth surfaces cause more friction.

3 A screw is a rolled-up slope.

4 Elastic materials stretch but do not go back to their original size and shape.

5 On Earth, things have weight because gravity pulls them down to the ground.

6 In a clock, gear wheels make the big hand and the little hand turn at the same speed.

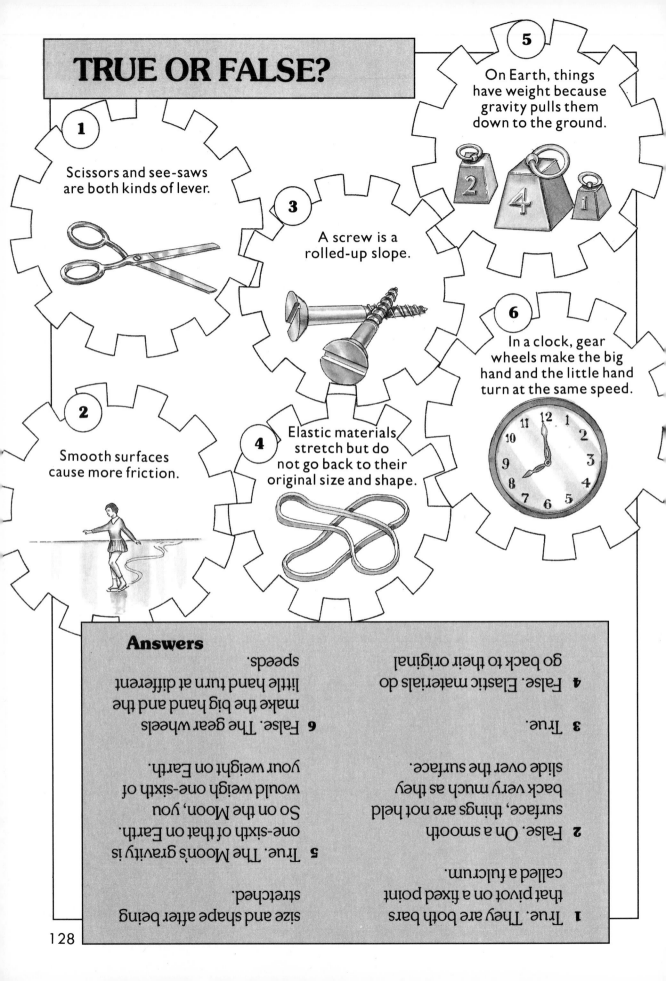

Answers

1 True. They are both bars that pivot on a fixed point called a fulcrum.

2 False. On a smooth surface, things are not held back very much as they slide over the surface.

3 True.

4 False. Elastic materials do go back to their original size and shape after being stretched.

5 True. The Moon's gravity is one-sixth of that on Earth. So on the Moon, you would weigh one-sixth of your weight on Earth.

6 False. The gear wheels make the big hand and the little hand turn at different speeds.

Sound and Music

Does sound travel faster through water or through air?
How many decibels is normal conversation? How do
stethoscopes help doctors to hear inside the human body?
If you blow across the top of a short straw, does it produce
a higher or a lower note than a long straw? How do
recorders produce lots of different notes? Why are two ears
better than one?

This section will help you to discover the answers to these
questions and has lots of ideas for ways to investigate
sound and music.

SOUND AND MUSIC

In this section, you can discover how we hear sounds and find out how to make music by plucking strings, blowing down pipes and hitting percussion instruments, such as drums.

The section is divided into seven different topics. Look out for the big headings with a circle at each end – like the one at the top of this page. These headings tell you where a new topic starts.

Pages 132–137

Sounds all Around

Everyday sounds; what is sound?; how sound travels through solids, water or air.

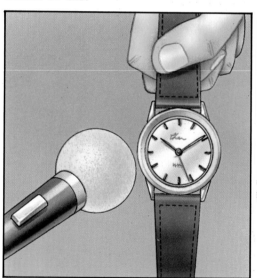

Pages 138–143

Loud and Quiet Sounds

Decibel scale; testing your hearing; megaphones and stethoscopes.

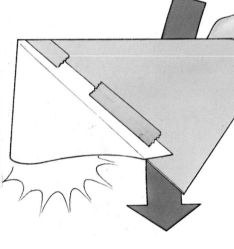

Pages 144–151

Drums, Scrapers, Shakers

Percussion instruments: drums; xylophones; chimes; maracas.

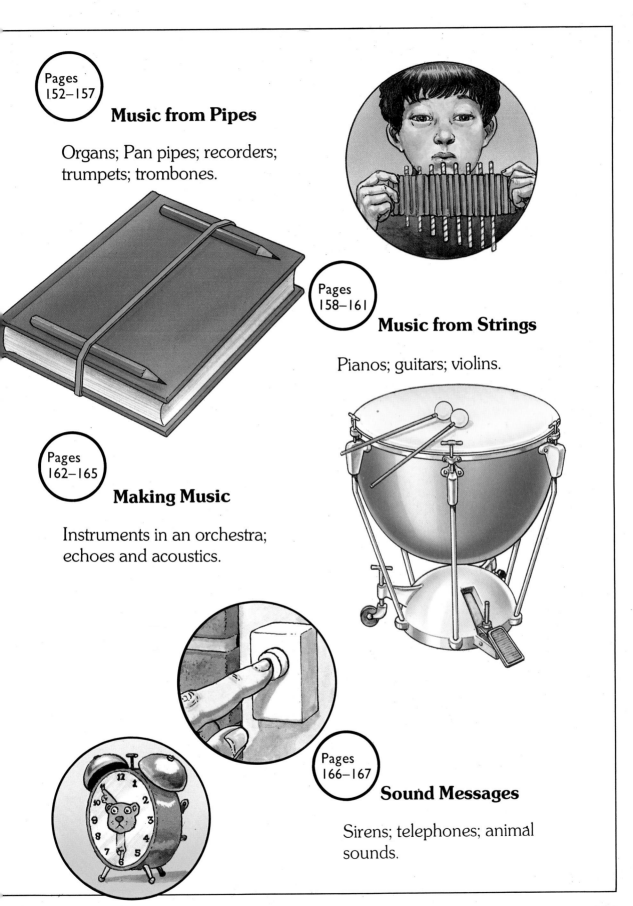

SOUNDS ALL AROUND

Make a tape recording of the everyday sounds around you. You could include sounds such as a door banging, a clock ticking, a bell ringing or the sounds made by people, pets or traffic. Try to record sounds indoors and out of doors.

Play the tape back to a friend. Can they recognize all the different sounds? Can you think of words to describe the sounds? Make up a poem or a story which includes all the sounds on the tape.

▶ In a noisy place, such as a fairground, it is hard to pick out separate sounds.

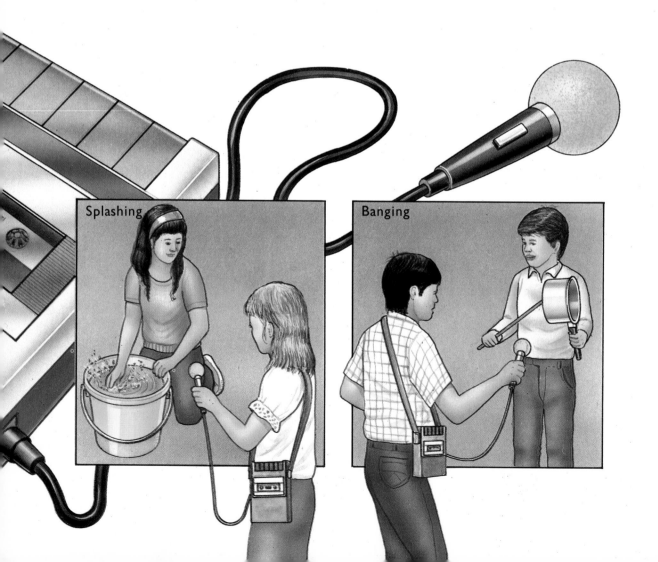

Splashing

Banging

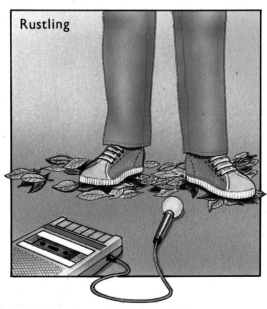
Rustling

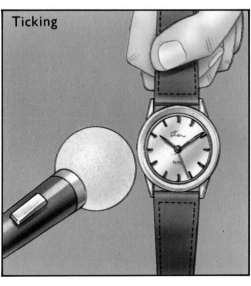
Ticking

133

Making Sounds

Make a collection of different materials, such as tissue paper, sandpaper, foil, cardboard, wood, plastic, sponge and glass. Put up a screen and ask your friends to sit on one side of the screen. On the other side of the screen, make sounds with the materials in your collection. How many different ways of making sounds can you discover? Can your friends guess which materials you are using each time?

Sound on the Move

Find a long length of iron railings and ask a friend to stand at one end while you stand at the other end. When your friend taps the railings with a stick, can you hear the sound? Now put your ear close to the railings and repeat the experiment. What happens to the sound?

 **Sounds Underwater**

Blow up a balloon and hold it next to your ear. Hold a watch on the other side of the balloon. Can you hear the watch ticking? Now fill the balloon with water and repeat the experiment. Does the water make the sound louder or quieter?

Sound travels about five times faster through water than it does through air. The sound of the watch should be louder through the water-filled balloon.

What Happens
Sounds travel faster through solid materials, such as the iron railings, than they do through air. So when you put your ear to the railings, the sound seems much louder. Try the same experiment with a brick wall instead of iron railings. You could make up a code of long and short taps and send messages.

Feeling Sounds

Sounds are invisible. You can't see them. But you can feel the way sounds make the air shake to and fro. These shaking movements are called vibrations. Rest two fingers lightly against your throat and say something. Can you feel the sound vibrations? When something vibrates fast, it makes high sounds. When something vibrates more slowly, the sounds are lower.

To feel the sounds made by a radio or cassette recorder, blow up a balloon and hold it in front of the loudspeakers. Compare the vibrations made by different kinds of music and loud and quiet music. Do the vibrations feel different?

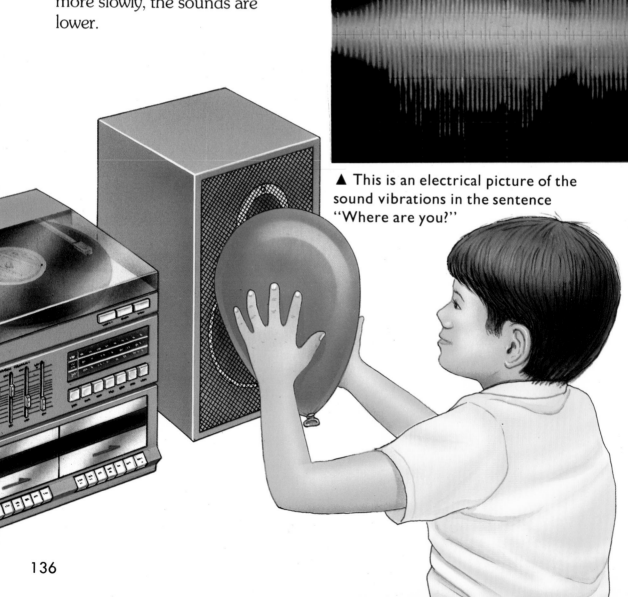

▲ This is an electrical picture of the sound vibrations in the sentence "Where are you?"

Seeing Sounds

To see a picture of your voice, try this experiment.

You will need:

a balloon, scissors, a short cardboard tube, an elastic band, a small piece of foil, a torch, glue, a plain wall or piece of card.

1. Cut off the neck of the balloon and stretch the rest of the balloon tightly over one end of the tube. Use the elastic band to hold the balloon in place.
2. Glue the small piece of foil on to the balloon skin.
3. Shine the torch on to the foil at an angle so you can see a bright spot of light reflected on to the wall or card.
4. Speak into the open end of the tube. Try high and low sounds as well as loud and quiet sounds. What happens to the light spot?

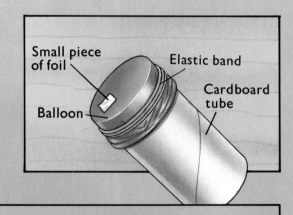

Small piece of foil
Elastic band
Cardboard tube
Balloon

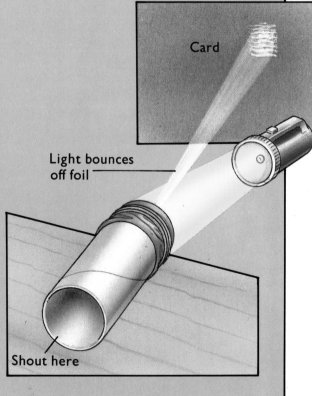

Card

Light bounces off foil

Shout here

What happens

The vibrations from your voice make the air in the tube vibrate. The air vibrations make the balloon skin and the reflected light vibrate too. You see the vibrations as streaks and wavy lines on the light spot.

LOUD AND QUIET SOUNDS

What is the loudest sound you have ever heard? Was it made by an aeroplane, a siren, or thunder during a storm? How many quiet sounds can you think of? Here are some ideas to get you started: footsteps on the carpet, a ticking watch, a mouse squeaking.

Draw a chart of objects that make loud sounds and objects that make quiet sounds. Do the objects in each group have anything in common?

The loudness of a sound is measured in units called decibels. Here is the decibel scale *(right)*. Did you know that a humpback whale can make a noise louder than Concorde on take-off? (190 decibels)

Decibel Scale	
0	humans can just hear sounds
10	rustling leaves
20	whisper
60	normal conversation
80	heavy traffic
100	pneumatic drill
110	disco
120	jet aircraft

▶ We call sounds we don't want or don't like noise. Very loud noise can damage our ears. People who work in noisy places should wear ear muffs to protect their ears.

Make your own ear muffs from foil cake cases or empty boxes. Hold them over your ears or use a hair band, elastic bands or shoe laces to fix them in position. To cut out even more noise, try padding out the inside of the ear muffs with cotton wool, paper or tissue.

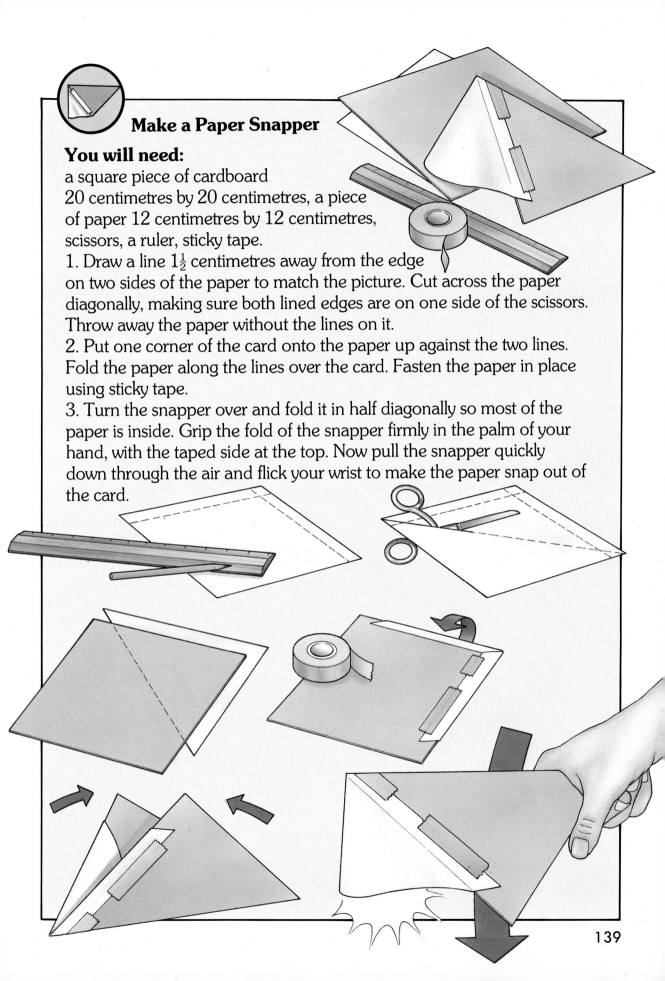

Make a Paper Snapper

You will need:

a square piece of cardboard
20 centimetres by 20 centimetres, a piece
of paper 12 centimetres by 12 centimetres,
scissors, a ruler, sticky tape.

1. Draw a line $1\frac{1}{2}$ centimetres away from the edge
on two sides of the paper to match the picture. Cut across the paper
diagonally, making sure both lined edges are on one side of the scissors.
Throw away the paper without the lines on it.

2. Put one corner of the card onto the paper up against the two lines.
Fold the paper along the lines over the card. Fasten the paper in place
using sticky tape.

3. Turn the snapper over and fold it in half diagonally so most of the
paper is inside. Grip the fold of the snapper firmly in the palm of your
hand, with the taped side at the top. Now pull the snapper quickly
down through the air and flick your wrist to make the paper snap out of
the card.

How Well Can You Hear?

Can you hear a pin drop? Ask a friend to stand with their back to a table and drop a pin on to the table. If they can hear the sound, they should put up one hand. Ask your friend to move away from the table two paces at a time until they can no longer hear the pin drop. Use a ruler to make sure you drop the pin from the same height each time. How far away can they still hear the pin?

Now try dropping a coin on to a different surface, such as carpet, grass, concrete, wood or metal. On which material does the coin make the loudest sound? Make a list of all the materials. Arrange the list in order from the loudest to the quietest materials.

Animal Hearing

Most people can hear sounds from about 20 to 17,000 vibrations per second. But some animals can hear higher or lower sounds than we can. Dogs can hear the sounds made by special whistles, and cats can hear the squeaks of mice, which are too high for us to hear.

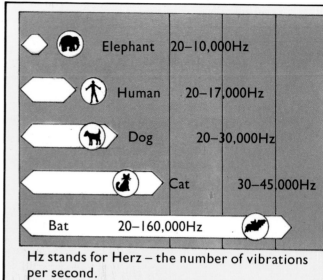

Elephant	20–10,000Hz		
Human	20–17,000Hz		
Dog		20–30,000Hz	
Cat			30–45,000Hz
Bat	20–160,000Hz		

Hz stands for Herz – the number of vibrations per second.

Two Ears are Better than One

To work out the direction of a sound, we compare the loudness of the sound reaching each ear. Some animals, such as rabbits, can swivel their ears to listen to sounds. This helps them to escape danger. Can you move your ears?

Can you guess the direction of a sound made by a friend when you are wearing a blindfold? The blindfold will help you to concentrate on the sounds. Try the same test with one ear covered. Are two ears better than one? Can you hear better with one ear than the other?

Making Sounds Louder

Cup your hands and hold them behind your ears. Can you hear better with your big ears? Now try holding your hands in front of your ears with the palms facing backwards. Can you hear the sounds behind you more easily? How many animals can you think of with big ears?

Make a Stethoscope

Push a plastic funnel on to each end of a long piece of plastic or rubber tubing. Then ask a friend to hold one funnel over their chest while you hold the other funnel to your ear. Can you hear your friend's heart beating?
A doctor uses a stethoscope like this to listen to sounds inside the body. This helps the doctor to find out about a person's health.

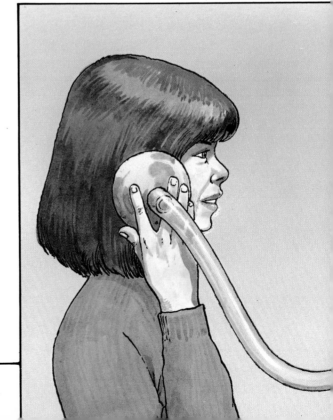

Making a Trumpet . . . and a Megaphone

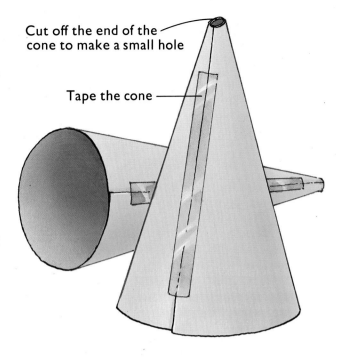

Cut off the end of the cone to make a small hole

Tape the cone

Make an ear trumpet by rolling a large sheet of paper into a cone shape. Hold the thin end of the trumpet to your ear. The cone collects sounds and makes them seem louder. With an ear trumpet in each ear, can you hear twice as well? Do large trumpets work better than small ones? How many musical instruments can you think of which include a trumpet?

To make a megaphone out of your trumpet, simply shout into the narrow end. The cone traps the sound of your voice and makes it seem louder.

Ask a friend to shout into a megaphone while you listen with an ear trumpet. How far away can you hear the sound of your friend's voice?

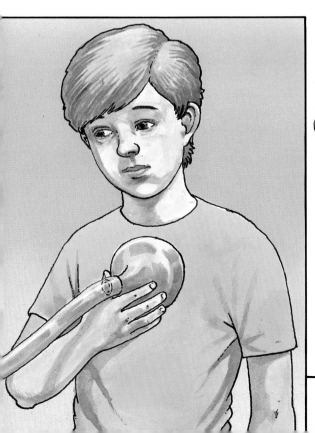

Instead of funnels, ask an adult to cut off the tops of two plastic bottles, as shown here.

DRUMS, SCRAPERS, SHAKERS

Many musical instruments produce sounds when they are hit. These are called percussion instruments. The name comes from the word 'percuss', which means to strike. They include drums, cymbals, triangles, tambourines and xylophones.

 Making Drums

You can use a box or any hollow container as a drum. But to make a drum that gives out different notes, you need a drumskin. Cut a piece out of a plastic bag and stretch it over a plastic bowl. Use tape or string to hold the bag in place. If you stretch the skin tighter, the plastic skin will vibrate faster and make a higher note.

Try making a drumskin from different materials, such as cloth, a balloon or paper soaked in wallpaper paste to make it go hard. Which materials make the best sounds? Which materials last longest?

Try putting a few grains of rice on top of the drum. When you tap the drum, the sound makes the drum shake and the rice jumps up in the air. When the drum-skin is stretched tighter, does the rice jump higher in the air?

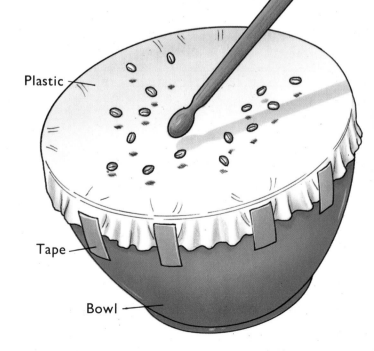

Plastic

Tape

Bowl

▲ Kettle drums or timpani have screws or a pedal to tighten the skin and change the note.

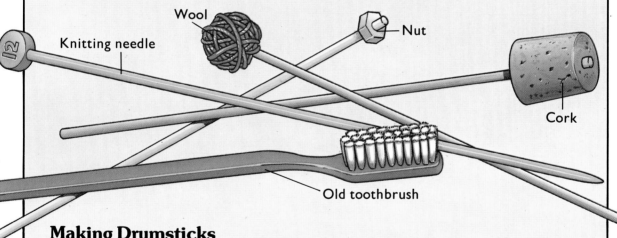

Making Drumsticks

You can make different sounds with the same drum by using different ends on the drumsticks. Here are some ideas to try:
wooden beads, cork, a cloth, wool, sponge, a nut, bristles from a toothbrush or a hairbrush.
Fix the ends to the drumsticks with tape or elastic bands. Cloth or sponge ends make a quiet sound. Beads make a louder sound. What sort of sound do the bristles make? Which sound do you like best?

This West African drum is called a waisted drum because it has a narrow 'waist' in the middle. By pressing on the lacing that joins the two skins, the drummer can change the note.

Make a Prayer Drum

1. Soak the brown paper in the paste and leave it to dry.
2. In the sides of the box or tub, cut two holes opposite each other and push the stick or dowel through the holes. Hold the wood in place with tape or clay.
3. Make two small holes in the other sides of the box. Thread one piece of string through each hole and tie a knot to keep the string in place.
4. Cut off the bottom of the box or tub.
5. To make the drumskins, tape a piece of the brown paper over each end of the box.
6. Pull each string across the drumskins in turn and mark where it reaches the middle. Tie a bead on to the string at this point.
7. Paint the sides of the drum with a pattern that you like, and leave it to dry.
8. To play the drum, twist the stick between your fingers so the beads hit the drumskin.

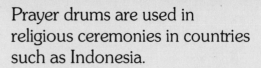

Prayer drums are used in religious ceremonies in countries such as Indonesia.

You will need:
a round, wooden box or a round plastic margarine tub, strong brown paper 30 centimetres by 30 centimetres, wallpaper paste, sticky tape, string, two wooden beads, dowel or a stick, a pencil, paints and paintbrushes, scissors, modelling clay.

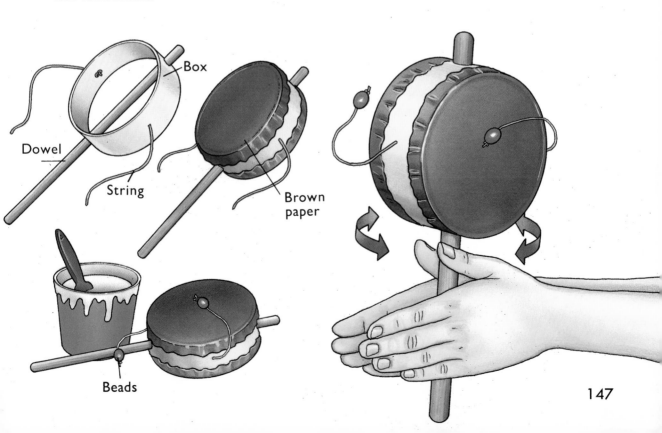

Box

Dowel

String

Brown paper

Beads

Making Scrapers

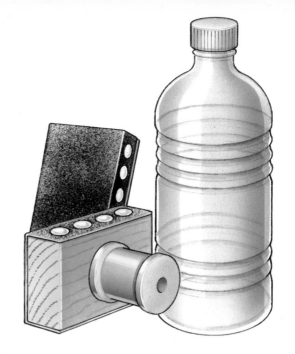

A plastic bottle with ridges along the sides makes a good scraper. Try using different objects, such as metal spoons, pencils or stones to scrape along the ridges.

You can make another kind of scraper from two wooden blocks with sandpaper pinned on top. To make a handle for each scraper, glue a cotton reel to the back of the block. Paint the back of the scrapers with bright patterns. To make scraping sounds, hold one block in each hand and rub the sandpaper sides together.

Make different sized pairs of scrapers. How are the sounds different? Try sticking the sandpaper to hollow boxes instead of solid blocks of wood. You should be able to make louder sounds.

Make a Nail Xylophone

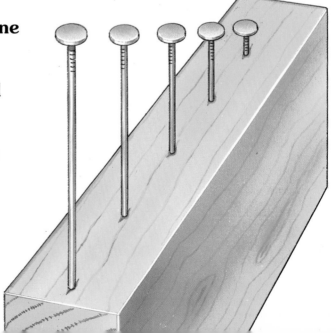

Ask an adult to help you bang some nails into a piece of wood so they stick out at different heights. Tap each nail with a metal spoon. Which nail makes the highest note? Which nail makes the lowest note?

Making Chimes

Make a set of chimes by hanging different objects from a length of string or a piece of wood. Try objects such as metal spoons or saucepans, a wooden ruler, a plastic bottle and a mug. Tap each object gently with a stick. How does the size of each object affect the note it gives out?

Shake, Rattle and Roll

A shaker can be made from empty plastic bottles, margarine cartons or small boxes. Collect containers that are different shapes and sizes and make sure they are clean and dry inside. Fill each container with small objects that will rattle around inside.

Fix the lid on the container with sticky tape and paint your shaker or cover it with wrapping paper. Which fillings make the loudest sound?

Here are some ideas for the fillings:

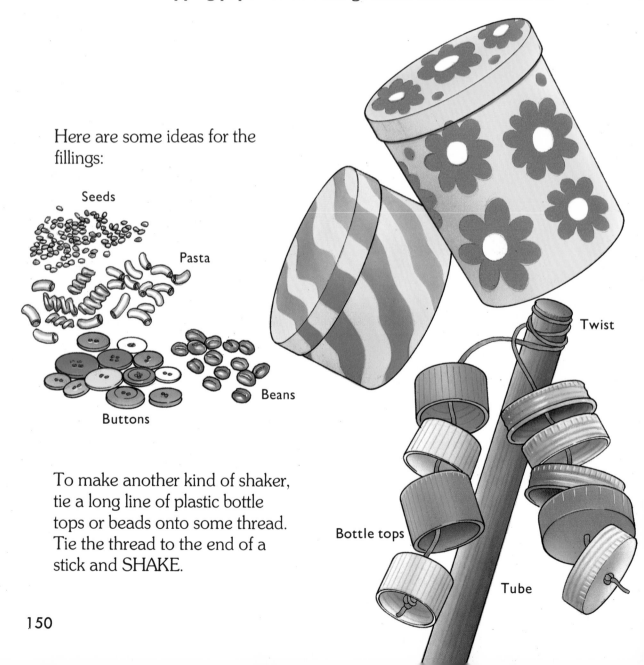

Seeds

Pasta

Beans

Buttons

Twist

Bottle tops

Tube

To make another kind of shaker, tie a long line of plastic bottle tops or beads onto some thread. Tie the thread to the end of a stick and SHAKE.

Making Maracas

1. Make small cuts around one end of the tube so it opens out flat. Glue this end to the bottom of one of the cups.
2. Pour the beans into the other cup.
3. Fix the two cups firmly together with plenty of sticky tape so the beans can't escape.
4. Paint or colour the cardboard tube.
5. Hold the cardboard tube and shake to make a sound.
6. Make another one and shake your maracas in time with your favourite music.

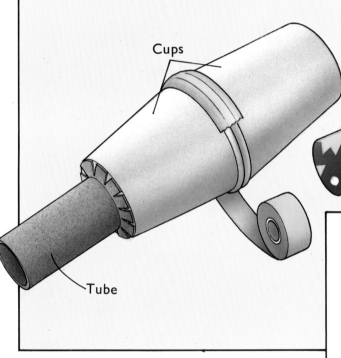

Cups

Tube

You will need:

two paper cups, a cardboard tube, dried beans, scissors, sticky tape, glue, paints or crayons.

Guess what's inside

Find a bottle you can't see through and choose one sort of filling to put inside. Can your friends guess what is inside the shaker?

MUSIC FROM PIPES

If you blow across the top of an empty bottle, you can make a musical note. This happens because you are making the air inside the bottle shake or vibrate. Musical instruments such as recorders, organs or trumpets work in a similar way. The player blows into the end of a pipe and this makes the air vibrate and give out musical sounds.

Make a Bottle Organ

1. Collect several clean, glass bottles that are all the same size and shape.
2. Put the bottles in a line.
3. Fill one bottle with water almost to the top. Leave some air above the water.
4. Put a little less water in the next bottle and so on down the line. The last bottle should have just a small amount of water in the bottom.
5. Blow across the top of each bottle. Which bottle makes the highest note? Which bottle makes the lowest note?
6. With a metal spoon, tap each bottle gently. What happens to the notes?
7. Can you play a tune on your bottles? It is a good idea to put a number on each bottle. Then you can write down your music.

Singing Bottles

Find two clean, empty glass bottles that are exactly the same size and shape. Ask a friend to hold one of the bottles to their ear. Then stand about one metre away and blow across the top of the other bottle. What can your friend hear?

The vibrations of the air in your bottle trigger the same vibrations in your friend's bottle. So they should hear a faint note in their bottle. This is called resonance.

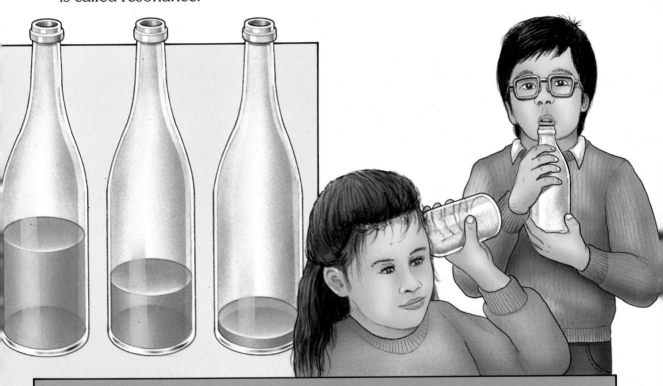

What Happens

When you blow across a bottle with a small amount of air inside, the air vibrates quickly and makes a high note. With more air in the bottle, the air vibrates more slowly and the note is lower.

When you tap the bottles, you make the water vibrate instead of the air. So the notes are the opposite way round. The bottles with a small amount of water give out high notes and the bottles with a lot of water give out low notes.

 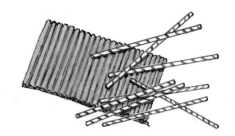

Make Pan Pipes

Pan pipes are a set of pipes that are played by blowing across the top. They are named after the Greek god Pan, who was half man and half goat. The music from his pipes was supposed to have power over all animals. The organ was probably developed from Pan pipes.

You will need:
a thin strip of corrugated cardboard, eight straws, scissors.

1. Push a straw through every other opening in the cardboard.
2. Cut each straw a different length with the longest straw at one end and the shortest straw at the other end. Make sure you have an even, sloping line, which matches the picture.
3. To play your Pan pipes, blow across the tops of the straws. Which straw makes the highest note? Which straw makes the lowest note?

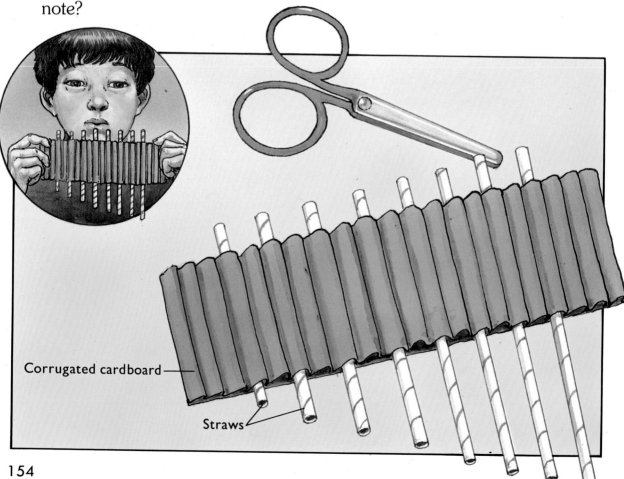

Corrugated cardboard

Straws

▲ If one pipe makes one note, how do instruments such as recorders make lots of different notes? A recorder has small holes along the pipe. When the player covers all the holes with their fingers, they are using one long pipe. When they take one or more fingers off the holes, they make the pipe shorter. This means they can play different notes.

Sound from Grass

Blade of grass

Hold a thick blade of grass tightly between your thumbs and blow hard. Can you make a screeching noise? The grass vibrates to produce the sound. This is what happens when a person blows on a reed in a musical instrument. Such instruments were originally all made of wood, and they are all played by the breath of the person, so they are called woodwind instruments.

Musical Straws

1. Flatten the end of a straw and snip the end to make two points or 'reeds'. Now blow hard between the two reeds to set the air in the straw vibrating.
2. Keep blowing through the reeds while you snip off bits from the other end of the straw. What happens to the note?
3. To make a straw play two notes, cut a hole in one side of the middle of the straw. Bend the straw down to play a different note.

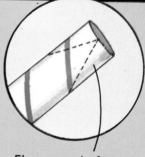

Flatten end of straw

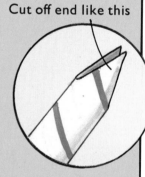

Cut off end like this

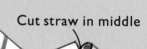

Cut straw in middle

Make a Trombone

Purse your lips and make a noise down a piece of plastic piping. Keep making the noise as you lift the pipe up and down in a bucket of water. How does the sound change?

A real trombone player pushes a slide on the side of the instrument up and down to change the length of the tube.

▼ Instruments made from brass, such as this trumpet, do not have reeds inside them. Instead, the player uses his own lips as reeds. When his lips are pressed tightly together, the air vibrates rapidly and produces a high note. He makes lower notes with his lips pressed loosely together.

MUSIC FROM STRINGS

Stretch an elastic band around a book and put two pencils under the band. Pluck the band to make it vibrate and produce a sound. First try with the pencils a long way apart. Then move the pencils closer together. With a shorter length of band to vibrate, you will produce a higher note.

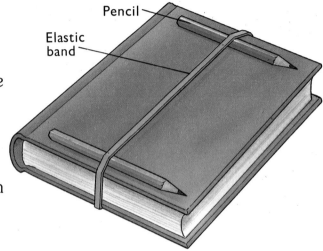

Pencil

Elastic band

Musical instruments that produce sound by vibrating strings are called stringed instruments. Some, such as the guitar, are played with the fingers. Others, such as the violin, are played with a bow.

Pinging Strings

1. Ask an adult to help you knock the nails into the wood to match the picture.
2. Pull one elastic band around each pair of nails.
3. Pluck the elastic bands with your fingers. Which bands make high sounds? Which bands make low sounds?

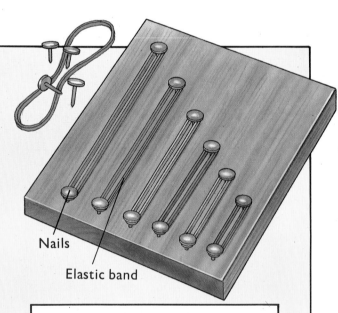

Nails

Elastic band

You will need:

a thick piece of wood, a hammer, some short nails, six elastic bands all the same size and thickness.

Make a Guitar

Collect together a large plastic box and eight elastic bands. Try to find long and short bands as well as thick and thin ones. Stretch the bands around the box and pluck them to make musical notes. Do the thin bands make higher or lower notes than the thick bands? If you use a bigger box or a smaller box, how does this change the notes?

What Happens

The vibrations of the bands make the air inside the box vibrate. And this, in turn, makes a lot of air around the box vibrate too. So you hear louder notes than from a solid piece of wood. This is why instruments with strings have a hollow box underneath the strings.

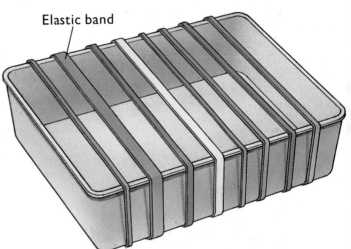

Elastic band

▼ Did you know that a piano makes music by vibrating strings? When the piano keys are pressed, little hammers hit wires inside the piano. This makes the wires and the whole piano case vibrate. The piano case makes the air around the piano vibrate too so it works like a giant sound box.

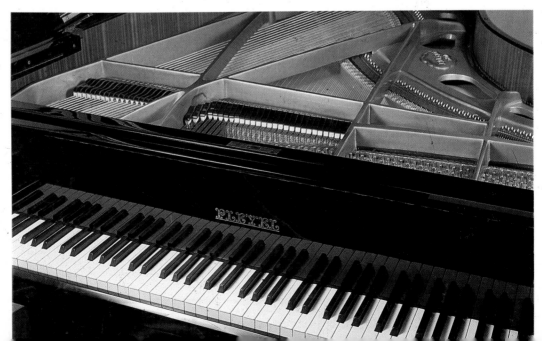

Stretching Strings

1. Ask an adult to help you hammer the nail into the wood to match the picture.
2. Tie one end of the string to the nail.
3. Ask an adult to hold the piece of wood securely on a table. Put some marbles or stones into the bucket and tie this to the other end of the string.
4. Put the pencils underneath the string to lift it clear of the wood.
5. Pluck the string and listen to the note.
6. Now put some more marbles or stones into the bucket so the string is stretched tighter.
7. Pluck the string again. Is the note higher or lower this time?

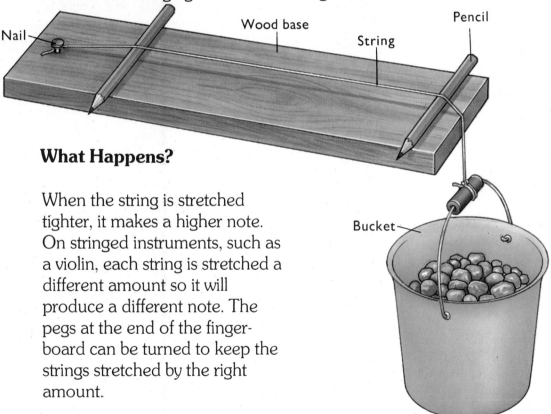

Nail

Wood base

String

Pencil

Bucket

What Happens?

When the string is stretched tighter, it makes a higher note. On stringed instruments, such as a violin, each string is stretched a different amount so it will produce a different note. The pegs at the end of the finger-board can be turned to keep the strings stretched by the right amount.

◄ If you watch someone playing a violin, you will see that they often press the strings down with their fingers. This makes the vibrating part of the string shorter so it makes a higher note.

MAKING MUSIC

In an orchestra, the musicians make air vibrate to produce musical notes in three main ways – with strings, with pipes or by hitting surfaces. Small instruments make high notes and large instruments make low notes.

In the picture, can you find examples of the different kinds of instruments? Look for stringed instruments (such as violin, cello and piano), woodwind instruments (such as clarinet, flute and bassoon), brass instruments (such as trumpet, trombone and french horn) and percussion instruments (such as cymbals, drum and triangle).

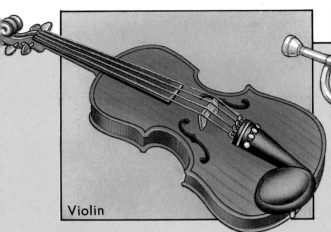

Violin

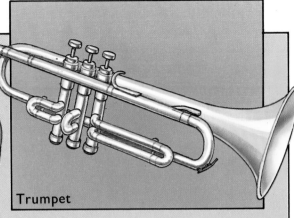

Trumpet

With Strings

In a stringed instrument, the note depends on the size and length of the string and how tightly it is stretched.

With Pipes

In woodwind and brass instruments, the note depends on the length of the pipe and the materials it is made from.

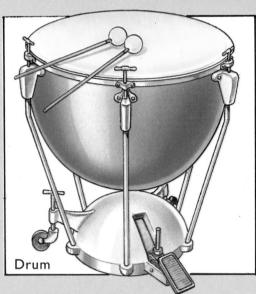

Drum

By Hitting Things

In percussion instruments, sounds are produced by striking with a special stick or hammer, or by hitting together the instruments themselves. Many of the instruments cannot produce definite notes but some can be tuned.

Sound Bounces Back

Try shouting into an empty bucket. Your voice bounces back from the sides of the bucket and the echoes sound very loud. In a concert hall or recording studio, the echoes can make it hard to hear the music properly. So the walls are usually lined with something that soaks up the sound. Cork, wood or heavy curtains are good materials for this job.

▼ In the Royal Albert Hall, London, discs in the ceiling help to reduce the echoes and make sound bounce back down to the audience.

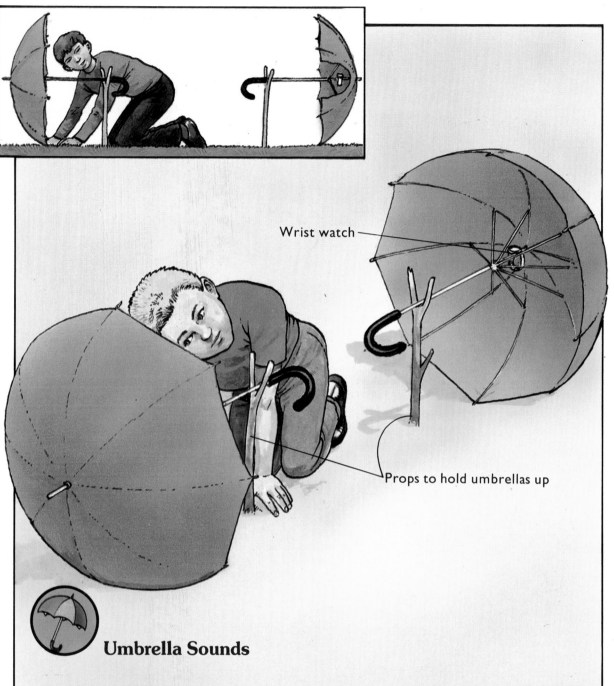

Wrist watch

Props to hold umbrellas up

Umbrella Sounds

To investigate the way sound bounces off things, try this test.
Arrange two umbrellas to match the picture. Make sure that the handles
of the umbrellas are in a straight line. Fix a watch to the handle of one
umbrella and put your ear to exactly the same point on the other
umbrella. The sound bounces from one umbrella to the other in a
straight line and very little sound is lost along the way. So you should be
able to hear the watch ticking.

SOUND MESSAGES

Sounds gives us all sorts of information about our surroundings. The sounds people make tell us when they are happy, sad, angry or frightened. Some sounds, such as music, are nice to listen to and may help us to relax. Other sounds, such as a police siren, carry an urgent warning message.

▲ Fire engines need to get to a fire as soon as possible. They use a loud bell or a siren to warn other vehicles and people to keep out of their way.

▼ The sound of a bell ringing is very useful for carrying messages. When a telephone rings, we know someone wants to speak to us. When a door bell rings, we know there is someone at the door. When an alarm clock rings, we know it is time to get up. Can you think of any other ways that we use bells to give us information?

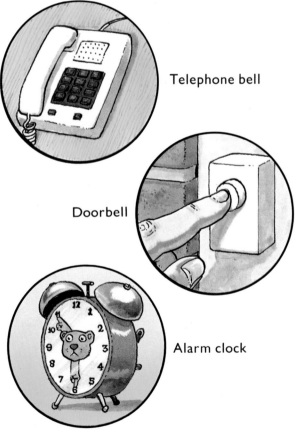

Telephone bell

Doorbell

Alarm clock

▲ A rattlesnake makes a loud, buzzing sound by shaking the 'rattle' at the end of its tail. This helps to scare off enemies, such as foxes. The rattle is made of old pieces of skin from the tip of the tail. The skin is hard, dry and hollow. Each time the snake sheds its skin, another piece is added to the rattle.

▶ Frogs make loud calls by moving air to and fro across the vocal cords in the throat. When they push air against the floor of the mouth, it expands like a balloon. The air in the 'balloon vibrates and helps to make the sounds louder. Frogs call to attract a mate and recognize others of their own kind.

TRUE OR FALSE?

1 Sound travels more slowly through solid materials than it does through air.

2 Blowing across a bottle top with a little air inside makes a high note.

3 When a short elastic band is plucked, it produces a lower note than a long elastic band.

4 A sound box makes the notes on a musical instrument louder.

5 A stretched string produces a high note.

6 Frogs make loud calls to attract insects for their supper.

Answers

1 False. Sound travels faster through solid materials than through air. This is because the particles or molecules which make up solids are closer together than they are in air.

2 True. The air vibrates quickly, producing a high note.

3 False. A shorter band vibrates quickly, producing a high note.

4 True. Sound boxes increase the amount of vibrating air, and so make sounds louder.

5 True. Stretched strings vibrate faster than looser ones.

6 False. Frogs call to attract a mate or to recognize others of their own kind.

168

GLOSSARY

Axle The rod on which a wheel turns.

Ball bearings Small steel balls used to reduce friction and help parts of machines move more easily.

Centre of gravity The place where the weight of an object seems to be concentrated. It is sometimes called the balancing point.

Decibel (dB) A unit used to measure the loudness of sound. Normal conversation is about 60 decibels and the sound of a jet engine is about 120 decibels.

Density The mass or 'weight' of a substance per unit of volume. In other words, how heavy something is for its size.

Displacement The amount of water or other liquid pushed out of the way by a floating object. If an object weighs the same as the liquid it displaces, it will float. If the object weighs more than the maximum amount of water it can displace, it will sink.

Echo A sound which has bounced off or been reflected from a surface, so you can hear it again.

Eclipse An eclipse of the Sun (Solar eclipse) occurs when the Moon stops sunlight from reaching the Earth. An eclipse of the Moon (Lunar eclipse) occurs when the Earth stops sunlight from reaching the Moon.

Elastic material A material that stretches, but goes back to its original shape after the stretching force is removed.

Filter A screen that stops things from passing through it.

Force A push or a pull that makes an object change its speed, direction or shape.

Friction A force that occurs when two surfaces rub against each other. It tends to slow things down or to stop them moving, and it produces heat.

Fulcrum The point at which a lever pivots or turns.

Gear wheels Wheels with teeth around the edge which fit together. Such wheels can act to change the speed or direction of movement.

Gravity The force of attraction between any two objects that have mass. (Mass is the amount of 'stuff' a body contains.) Gravity pulls everything on Earth down to the ground and gives things weight.

Hydrometer An instrument for measuring the density of liquids.

Kaleidoscope A tube through which patterns of symmetrical reflections can be seen.

Lever A bar or pole that swings or pivots on a fixed point called a **fulcrum**.

Liquid A runny substance which has no shape. It takes on the shape of the container it is in.

Maracas Club-like percussion instruments filled with beans. They are played by shaking.

Materials The substances from which things are made.

Megaphone A large trumpet-shaped instrument for carrying the sound of a voice over a distance.

Mirror A smooth, shiny surface that produces good reflections.

Opaque Something that does not allow light to pass through it. You cannot see through opaque materials.

Percussion instruments Musical instruments played by striking, shaking or scraping. They include drums, xylophones, guiros and maracas.

Periscope An instrument which uses the light reflected between mirrors in a tube to allow people to see things otherwise out of sight.

Pollution The spoiling and poisoning of the environment with harmful substances.

Pulley A wheel with a groove around the edge for carrying a rope or a cable. It is used to help people lift heavy weights.

Reed A separate device fixed inside a woodwind instrument which makes the air vibrate to produce the sound. Clarinets and saxophones have one reed; all other woodwind instruments, such as oboes, have two reeds.

Reflections The way light rays bounce back from a surface. Everything reflects some light, but flat, smooth or polished surfaces produce the best reflections.

Resonance When the vibrations of a substance, such as the wood of a violin, match the vibrations of the air which produce the sound.

Screw A slope wrapped in a spiral around a central rod. It changes a turning force into a much greater straight line force.

Shadow A dark area which forms behind an object when it blocks out a source of light. Shadows are places where light does not shine.

Solar power Energy produced from the Sun's light and heat rays, which is usually turned into electricity.

Sound box A hollow box with an opening which is placed behind something producing a sound to make the sound louder.

Speed of sound Sound travels faster through solids or liquids than it does through air. The speed of sound in air is about 330 metres per second. The speed of sound through water is about 1430 metres per second.

Streamlined Something with a smooth, slim shape that cuts through air or water easily and makes movement faster.

Stringed instruments Musical instruments which produce sounds by vibrating strings. They include guitars, violins and sitars.

Surface tension The pulling force that holds together the surface of liquids such as water and

makes them appear to have a thin elastic 'skin'.

Symmetrical object An object that can be divided into two or more parts which are exactly the same.

Translucent Something that lets some light through but scatters the light. If you look through a translucent material, things look blurred.

Transparent Something that lets light go straight through it. You can see clearly through transparent materials.

Upthrust The upward pushing force produced when an object is placed in a liquid or a gas.

Vibration When something moves to and fro. Sounds are caused by the air vibrating very fast, causing changes in the pressure of the air.

Wedge Two slopes stuck back to back which can be pushed into a gap to force two objects apart.

Woodwind instruments Musical instruments originally made of wood. They are played by the breath or 'wind' of a person, which makes the air inside a tube vibrate. Woodwind instruments include the oboe, bassoon and flute.

INDEX

Page numbers in
italics refer to
illustrations or where
illustrations and text
occur on the same
page.

Answers to quiz on page 14:
These things float: duck, pumice stone.
These things sink: toothbrush, soap, comb.

Acknowledgements

The publishers wish to thank the following
artists for contributing to this book:
Peter Bull: page headings, pp.45, 139,
144/145, 147, 150/151, 158/159;
Peter Dennis (Linda Rogers Associates):
pp.30/31, 38, 42/43, 44, 46/47, 70–75, 81,
96/97, 114–121, 123, 134/135, 140–143,
154, 156/157, 164–167;
Kuo Kang Chen: pp.12/13, 28/29, 33, 40/41,
52/53, 60/61, 66/67, 76/77, 84/85, 92–93,
102–103, 108–113, 132/133, 136/137,
148/149, 152/153, 162/163;
John Scorey: pp.54–59, 63, 64, 68, 78–79,
80, 82, 86, 98–101, 106–107, 124–127.

The publishers also wish to thank the
following for providing photographs for this
book:
29 Courtesy, J.W. Automarine; 159, 164
A.G.E. FotoStock; 101 Michael Holford; 92
(*left*) Lesley Howling; 55, 65, 66, 69, 83
Hutchison Library; 167 Pat Morris; 122
NASA; 112 Courtesy NTN Bearings; 13, 23
Picturepoint; 18 Jane Placca; 145 Courtesy,
Premier Percussion; 21, 22 Quadrant; 164
Royal Albert Hall; 104, 106, 115 Science
Museum, London; 32, 136 Science Photo
Library; 87 Spectrum; 95, 97, 111
Supersport Photos; 45 Thames Water plc;
155, 159 Tim Woodcock; 25, 27, 53, 78,
126, 133, 138, 157, 166 ZEFA.